REVIEWS

924 Miles is inspiring, challenging, comical, and relatable to all who have ever wondered about their purpose in life. David Gates challenges mediocrity and stagnation while delineating between drifting through life as opposed to moving where The Lord leads. David Gates presents a book that is easy to read, yet difficult to put down. A must read!

- Adam West, Senior Director, Virginia Baptist Children's Home

924 Miles is an honest and transparent account of one man's journey toward closer intimacy with the Lord. But this is no simple autobiography; rather, it is a challenge for all to dive into the grace of God with reckless abandon. This heartfelt book by Gates is easy to read, convicting, and full of joy in the journey.

- Dr. William Coleman, Lead Pastor, Bedrock Church Roanoke

"Good stories come from people who want to make a difference." David Gates leads us to explore our God-given dreams and that each of us can make an impact in the world while recognizing that God is not just a lifeline but He is with us, in us and works through us!

-Shenna Massey, co-founder of Spark Conference, www.gotospark.com

924 Miles

Thoughts on Finding God and Living a Meaningful Life

Your Story Matters!

David

David Gates

Copyright © 2015 David Gates.

All rights reserved. No part of this book may be used or reproduced by any means, graphic, electronic, or mechanical, including photocopying, recording, taping or by any information storage retrieval system without the written permission of the publisher except in the case of brief quotations embodied in critical articles and reviews.

This book is a work of non-fiction. Unless otherwise noted, the author and the publisher make no explicit guarantees as to the accuracy of the information contained in this book and in some cases, names of people and places have been altered to protect their privacy.

WestBow Press books may be ordered through booksellers or by contacting:

WestBow Press
A Division of Thomas Nelson & Zondervan
1663 Liberty Drive
Bloomington, IN 47403
www.westbowpress.com
1 (866) 928-1240

Because of the dynamic nature of the Internet, any web addresses or links contained in this book may have changed since publication and may no longer be valid. The views expressed in this work are solely those of the author and do not necessarily reflect the views of the publisher, and the publisher hereby disclaims any responsibility for them.

Any people depicted in stock imagery provided by Thinkstock are models, and such images are being used for illustrative purposes only. Certain stock imagery © Thinkstock.

ISBN: 978-1-4908-7498-2 (sc)
ISBN: 978-1-4908-7499-9 (hc)
ISBN: 978-1-4908-7497-5 (e)

Library of Congress Control Number: 2015904893

Print information available on the last page.

WestBow Press rev. date: 03/26/2015

To my wife, my children, and the community around me that I've grown to love.

Contents

Foreword ix
Prologue: Why Silence Isn't an Option xi

Chapter 1: A Single Spark 1
Chapter 2: 924 Miles 4
Chapter 3: Only God 10
Chapter 4: Something Has to Give 17
Chapter 5: The Big Move 22
Chapter 6: Choosing To Live 27
Chapter 7: A Foot in the Door 31
Chapter 8: Getting In My Way 35
Chapter 9: Street Dogs 38
Chapter 10: Full Circle 43
Chapter 11: Camping With the Enemy 48
Chapter 12: It Takes a Village 52
Chapter 13: Sex and Roses 56
Chapter 14: Cup-a-day Christians 61
Chapter 15: Finding Favor 65
Chapter 16: Just Be Something 72
Chapter 17: Status Quo 76
Chapter 18: Don't Stop Dreaming 80
Chapter 19: Love of a Father 83
Chapter 20: Church Planting 87
Chapter 21: Not For Sell 91
Chapter 22: It's Really Going to Happen 95

Acknowledgements 99

Foreword

It was Augustine who wrote, "Our hearts are restless until they find their rest in God," and J. R. R. Tolkien who wrote "not all who wander are lost." I think that restlessness is an important indicator of a vibrant faith journey. If a Christian is not experiencing restlessness, then they have a very small conception of who God is.

The God that I worship, and the God who comes across through the life of David Gates, is a transcendent and majestic Being who is big enough to inspire mystery and authority. And yet, this God is also intensely personal, caring about every detail of our lives. This concept of a powerful, yet loving God, comes through these pages clearly as we journey with David through the ups and downs of his life.

I get the sense from *924 Miles*, that "restlessness" is at the core of David Gates' being. Not a restlessness in the sense of discontentment, but a restlessness that drives him to consistently pursue the will of God. David is not content with following Christ because someone says to. He is also not satisfied with pursuing Jesus in the way everyone else pursues Him. He is a thinker, a doer, and desires to pursue Christ authentically.

I also get the sense that although David Gates "wandered"—through different jobs, states, and churches—he never felt lost.

Instead, as you will soon find out, he looks back over his life, and like Solomon declares, that it is the Lord who directs a man's steps. (Prov. 16:9)

Finally, as you journey through this book with David Gates, I hope that you will notice the theme of intentionality. It is one thing to desire God and feel restless. It is an entirely different matter, to be led by that restlessness into the intentional pursuit of God. I hope, that like David, you will pursue Christ with your life. Not just an understanding of Christ, but pursue a relationship with Him. Because after all, like David Gates will tell you, it's not enough to feel restless if you never find God.

Daniel Ryan Day
author, *Ten Days Without*
Producer, *Dr James Dobson's Family Talk*
@danielryanday

Prologue

Why Silence Isn't an Option

Adam, a friend of mine, told me that God didn't deliver us so that we could remain silent. It was a simple statement but it couldn't be more true. God raises us up so that we can give Him the glory through our stories. I never knew that I would write a book, and I really never expected to actually publish one. Either way, I guess that kind of makes me an author now, and I'm telling my story because remaining silent isn't an option. It may be for some people, but I believe that anyone who has received the mercy, grace, and love that I've received from God can't remain silent. I don't think it's possible.

It's kind of like when you find that awesome restaurant downtown, or you just had the best cup of coffee of your life. You've got to tell your friends about that new coffee shop or whatever it is that just changed your life. I know that a cup of coffee doesn't really have the ability to be life-changing, but you want them to experience the same euphoria that you just experienced. You want them to enjoy the happiness that you've discovered. I know I just compared God to a cup of coffee, but if you're a coffee drinker like I am, then you'll understand.

If you continue reading, we will hit on topics including the church, serving the community, taking chances, failure, dreams, and eventually, success. The first couple of chapters in this book do little more than tell you who I am and a little about where I come from. If you can get past all of that, I believe the remainder of the book will change your perspective on your life, God, and the relationship between the two. You may find the first couple of chapters to be boring, and honestly, I'm okay with that. My story and any part of this book that talks about me is the least important part of the story as a whole. This is written as my memoir, but truth be told, I am just a supporting character in a bigger story—in God's story.

So, that's really it. That's why I wrote this book. A friend of mine, who also writes books, told me that I had to include a prologue. I didn't really feel like writing one, but he said it was important for you to understand why this book exists. So now you know. Thanks for buying my book and happy reading.

Chapter 1

A Single Spark

There's a point in everyone's life when things start to become really relevant. As children we spend most of our time learning the basics of life. We learn to feed ourselves, get dressed, count, and read. We develop into little humans, running around and playing as if nothing in the world matters outside of the here and now. But at some point we start to understand that there is a purpose to life. We learn that change happens, and through that change, we develop into adults who have choices to make.

My story becomes relevant in my early teenage years. This was the time in my life when I was trying to develop talents and skills, and learn new things. It was in my early teenage years that I developed an interest for music, more specifically composition. I guess it started a little further back than my teenage years. When I was around eight, I had written a poem for a project in English class, and the poem had been selected to be published in a collection of poetry by young poets. It was some sort of annual publication. So, I guess the first spark was then, when I wrote that poem. It was pretty bad, but the bar was set low because I was a kid.

Either way, it was a door that I walked through, and it started a series of events that led me to writing this book. I have two brothers, and one of them used to write songs and was big into music for a while. This was while we were teenagers. His interest in songwriting and music led me to explore the music world a bit more. Eventually I started writing songs, recording them, and even tried my hand at selling them at school. I started a band, and we even had a dozen or so live shows over a couple of years.

On top of having an interest in music, I also have some really amazing parents. They are the type of parents who would tell me I could do anything I wanted to. They were so supportive that at the age of fifteen, I applied to a music college to pursue my music career. Though I never became famous or a rock star, I did have a thing for composing, and I could see the interest slowly starting to transform into a true talent.

To my surprise, the most prestigious music college in the country actually took the time to reply to my application. They requested that I send some of my compositions to them before they would make any kind of decision, so that's exactly what I did. A couple of weeks went by, and I got a letter in the mail from Berklee College of Music. This was the big day I had been waiting for. I opened the letter and read it. Then I read it again to make sure I had read it correctly. I had just been accepted into music school. Looking back, it was much more exciting then. I was fifteen, loved to compose, and had just been accepted into a college to do just that!

I think I already mentioned that I had pretty awesome parents, but sometimes I wish they had just said, "Hey son, music is great and all, but you'll never make any money, so get a real degree." Harsh? Yeah, maybe so, but it would have saved me an additional four years of college, because I had to go back when my music education didn't lead to any real kind of income.

At the end of the day, I think the takeaway is much more than a music education or the ability to compose. I think it's learning that we all have a spark. A poem I wrote when I was eight years old led me to an interest in music and composition and then on to a music education, where I learned a lot about myself and what was important to me.

We all have a spark, but sometimes it is hidden deep inside of us. It's that thing inside of us that makes us come alive. It's hiding, and it's waiting to become a flame. Sometimes it takes something unexpected to find our spark. Sometimes it takes encouragement from family, a push from a friend, or a life-changing event to figure out what we are made of. At the end of the day, the spark is there, and it's alive. It just needs a bit of fanning.

Chapter 2

924 Miles

After graduating music school, I did what anybody who just spent nearly four years in a specialized school does: I went downtown and turned in my résumé at the local sheriff's office. After all, the music business wasn't as easy as I expected. I wasn't expecting to actually get an interview, since my only schooling was in music, and my only job experience was the seven months I spent as an assistant preschool teacher. I guess I did have six months as a labor hand at a sign-pressing shop too, but I was fifteen when I worked there, and it really wasn't much of a job. I went downtown and turned my résumé in because I could tell everyone thought it was a good idea, not because I really wanted to. I still had my mind set on music, but I was also three months away from my wedding day. Yes, I was fresh out of school, young, and in love.

It turns out the sheriff's office was in need of personnel, and they didn't have very many résumés on their desk. I not only got an interview but, in fact, I was hired the same day. This began my career in law enforcement. Shortly after starting the job, I did indeed marry the love of my life, and shortly after returning from the honeymoon, we even bought a house. Did I mention this all happened before I turned twenty? I was one of those guys, and still am in a way, who makes checklists and rarely misses a deadline. I had a five-year plan, and one year into it I was getting frighteningly close to finishing everything on the list.

The place where I grew up and later lived when my wife and I got married was a small, rundown town. It was one of those towns that a good murder novel might be set in. The businesses were failing, the school systems were below par, and the cool thing to do on the weekends was to catch up on the latest gossip. I didn't fit in, and I was set on not being stuck in this little town. I didn't want to sit idly after graduating school. I knew that if I lost momentum then I might never escape the mundane life that surrounded me.

Looking back, I think this is why I did so much so quickly. This is why I gave up parties and hanging out, to pick up college courses after high school each day. I was nineteen, had a steady job, a college education, and I married my high-school sweetheart. Check, check, and check. Now don't get the wrong idea; the marriage was the one thing on the list that wasn't just part of my plan for success. I was truly in love. I am truly in love.

As a kid, I always envisioned the shield and the gun as a safe haven. You know, they were the good guys. I wish I had found that to be entirely true. It's sad that more times than not, your childhood ideas of the world change when you grow up. A lot more happened over those three years too. Michaela and I had a daughter. There's much more to that story than just conception, pregnancy, and delivery, but we will get to that later on, minus the conception part.

During my tenure at the sheriff's office, I had lots of long days, and I was required to work every other weekend. This meant that we were only able to attend church twice a month, but let's face it, those were my two weekends off. Sleeping in felt better than sitting on a pew, so that's what we did.

I won't blame Michaela for any of that. Getting the family to church was my job, and most of the time I was the one who said that we should rest. I was successful at the sheriff's office. I made lieutenant in just under two years. On the flip side of this, our marriage was rocky even on the good days. Sometimes I wonder if our daughter was what kept us fighting through it. I had a bad habit of putting the job before my family, and even when I took time off, I was too drained from work to be good company to my family.

Needless to say, we were stuck in rut. We were looking for something to do, something to fill the spaces in our relationship and in our lives. One of the good things about the sheriff's office was that I had a decent income, and not a lot of bills. So we started buying things to fill the void. New furniture, barbecue pit, and even a motorcycle. It was a temporary fix.

After a week we were back in the same boat. Come to think of it, I should have bought a boat—or maybe not. It wasn't long before I became bored with the job. I started thinking about just resigning. We had a little money that we hadn't spent yet, and I could take a month or two off and find something else. So I drew up my resignation, and two weeks later I was unemployed.

You'd think that with the stress being lifted and the extra time with the family that we could patch things up. Now don't get the wrong idea, our marriage wasn't that bad off. We were just stuck. You know, that feeling when you don't feel any purpose in life. It was like we weren't accomplishing anything. We were just existing. The only new and exciting thing in our lives at the time was our daughter. And don't get me wrong, that was amazing in itself. We just needed something more. We had identified the problem, just not the solution.

I think the other thing that helped us out during this time, besides our shared love for our daughter, was that we did go back to church after Makenzie was born. Even with that, we were still searching for something else. We were suffocating and I was having trouble landing another job. So after a few months of being lazily unemployed, we decided to move.

We sold our house to a guy I worked with at the sheriff's office, packed up, and moved an hour away to a town called West Monroe, Louisiana. If I had written this book a few years ago, not a single bell or whistle would have gone off when I mentioned West Monroe. Now it's known as the *Duck Dynasty* town.

West Monroe was about an hour drive from where we grew up. It wasn't an expensive move, but it was an attempt at starting over. It was an attempt at something new. I figured I'd get a new job and hopefully a new perspective.

Though I was a bit discouraged by my experience in law enforcement, I figured that I'd give it another shot. I was hoping that this time would be different. We lived in West Monroe for eight months. It was a long eight months of job searching, working part-time for a security firm, and struggling to make ends meet. I lost count of the number of applications that I filled out.. I spent countless hours on different job search websites, and going door to door with resumes. However, during those eight months not everything was bad.

Michaela became pregnant with our son. There wasn't a bad way to view this. We wanted another child and God met that prayer with a son. However, we were on our way to having a two-year-old daughter, a newborn son, and a very unstable income. So at this point my job searching went from casual to frantic.

My dad is a veteran of the Navy. Even retired, he still serves as an instructor. My brother and my uncle both served in the Army. I had just spent three years working for a sheriff's office. It goes without saying that I am proud of the line of service in my family, and I felt that I needed to continue the tradition. I started applying for federal law enforcement jobs. I also talked to a Navy recruiter and a couple of other police departments. Out of all of my resumes and applications I sent in, I did receive a call for one of the positions. It was with the Department of Homeland Security and it was in Roanoke, Virginia. 924 miles away. I'm sure you can now guess the direction this story is going.

My dad and I drove the distance from Louisiana to Virginia so that I could take a few tests for the department, and on the way back to Louisiana I received an email. The email was short and to the point. They wanted to extend an offer of employment.

In just a couple of short weeks my family and I packed our house and prepared to move across the country.

There's something that was said to us right before we moved. It still plays in the back of my mind from time to time. As we were announcing the big move to our family, we received a bit of advice. We didn't ask for it, but it was given all the same. We were talking about the new possibilities, opportunities, and adventures waiting for us on the other side of the country. That's when it happened. You know, that piece of advice I was talking about. We were told that despite the change of venue and the fact that we were moving to a new place, that nothing would be different. We were told that even though we had always wanted to live in the mountains, that moving wasn't going to make our lives any better.

All of the excitement and the butterflies that I had felt over the past few weeks quickly went away, and out of the bottom of my stomach anger started to form. Who were they to rain on our parade? We had been stuck in a rut for years. We lived in a dead-end town with dead-end jobs, and there wasn't a single drop of diversity for miles.

To tell you the truth, that was the big problem. Everyone was just alike, thought just alike, and if you didn't follow suit, then you were the black sheep. But you see, all that the advice managed to do was send me into overdrive. Now failure wasn't an option. I would move across country, become successful, and live the life I'd been dreaming of; the life we'd been praying for.

I'd been praying for a while now. I wasn't living the life God had for me, but I wasn't living without Him either. I had been praying that God would open a door for a new beginning. I'd been praying that He would show me what He wanted us to do. I didn't know what else to do. I was out of options. So when this job opened up nearly a thousand miles away, I jumped at it. Finally a door had opened for me and my family.

Chapter 3

Only God

I mentioned earlier that I would get into my daughter's story. I think this is as good of a time as any. My wife and I had talked about having kids for a while. We talked about how long we wanted to me married before we tried to start a family. Most people just talk about it, make a plan, and start a family. For us it was different, or at least it was supposed to be different. My wife wasn't supposed to be able to have kids according to the doctors. Obviously trying to start a family wouldn't hurt anything, but we were hesitant because of the possibility of being let down. We were worried that the doctors would be right.

Eventually we decided that we would never know if we didn't try. We decided it was time to start a family. It only took a few months for us to get a positive pregnancy test. It was a strange mix of emotions. We were excited and thankful that the doctors were wrong, but we were also now faced with a pregnancy and the idea of becoming parents.

This story will take you on a roller coaster of emotions, or at least it is taking me there as I write it. Our first appointment went well. Everything looked good on the ultrasound. Things were going well, and we were one month closer to becoming parents. Then, through a series of events and hospital trips, we faced our first real challenge as newlyweds. We went to the hospital because things didn't seem right, and it turns out that they weren't.

After hours at the emergency room and a series of tests, we found ourselves faced with the reality that we had just lost our baby. Now, I know a lot of people will debate the exact moment a fetus becomes a child, but for me it was the moment we saw that positive pregnancy test. It wasn't a mistake we made and it wasn't a surprise. We wanted a child and Michaela had become pregnant. You can spin it any way you want when it's your pregnancy, but for us, we had just lost our child.

Until this point, the roller coaster was just building up the momentum to climb the first hill. You know, that steady click, click, click, to the top. The emotions had come and gone, the anticipation and fear mixed and grew larger. Just as we reached the top we realized that the drop was far higher and scarier than we ever imagined. I think this was when the anger started to harbor itself deep inside. It wasn't really directed, but it was real and it was ever present. It balanced our pain and depression. A hundred questions that would never be answered swam in our minds.

I've only yelled at God a few times. Even though none of them were warranted, this one felt the closest. You can judge me if you'd like. I yelled at God and it's hard for me to feel bad for doing it. I couldn't understand why God even gave us the pregnancy in the first place if He was just going to pull it out from under us. I figured God was a lot different than I ever imagined Him. Maybe he was twisted. Maybe he liked to see His people squirm a bit. Maybe He liked the control.

I was angry at the doctors who said we couldn't have kids, not because they did anything wrong, but because they had been right. They even made sure to maximize the pain at our follow up appointment. They suggested that we not try to conceive again. It was easy for them to say I guess. They'd become numb to the whole process. They were used to giving bad news, and then moving on to the next patient. I guess some of that resentment never faded. I was over having people tell me what was best for me. This began a weird period of my life. It brought me closer to God, but only because I needed something to hold on to. It also caused me to push away from him.

Michaela and I really wanted a child. We talked it over, and after a bit of crying, and yelling, and long nights, we decided that we weren't going to let other people decide whether we could be parents. Roughly six months later we decided that we wanted to try again at starting a family. We knew that if the same thing happened again that it might be too much to handle, but not being parents wasn't sitting well either.

A few months later we had another positive pregnancy test. This time the emotions didn't become overwhelming. I mean, we wanted to be excited and tell everyone, but we were scared. We were not only scared of losing another child, but also of the judgment from our family and friends. They knew we were told not to try again, and they'd be sure to mention it. This time we kept it a secret for a while.

Fast forward a few months and we had made it to what most people considered the safe point in the pregnancy. It was very unlikely to lose the baby. We told our friends and family. Even though things were going well, we were filled with worries and doubts from almost everyone around us.

You know, I remember someone at the church I used to attend who went through a miscarriage. At the time I was a teenager, and I didn't understand what a miscarriage was. I do recall the poor lady walking around with a twisted grimace on her face. I also remember that she got a lot of hugs. I get it now. I wish I had known then, because then maybe I could have said something nice to her. Maybe I could have made her feel a little better.

It is difficult to go through a traumatic experience in life, but there is still something worse. Going through something traumatic and having no one there in your corner is far worse. My biggest fear in life isn't death, or poverty, or sickness. My biggest fear is loneliness. I think that is something that most of us can relate to.

I'm not talking about isolating yourself behind a computer screen or being more of a phone kind of person. I mean truly being alone. There's no one to call, no one to talk to, and no one to love or to love you back.

This is why it hurts so badly when you are on a journey or going through a season of bad luck in your life and the people who are supposed to hold you up just don't get it. They don't get what you're experiencing, and instead of trying to understand, they just disconnect. That's kind of what we had happening. I don't want to give off the impression that no one was there for us, because we did have some family, and even a friend or two who stood beside us.

But I'll never forget when I returned to work after the miscarriage. A co-worker told me that the miscarriage was probably for the best because I was too young to be a parent anyway. I did everything I could to restrain from punching him in his face that day. I'm glad I didn't hit him since he was one of my supervisors.

So the pregnancy progressed, and despite the doubts and the increasingly annoying people throwing worries our way, things continued to go well. I was at work at the Sheriff's office one night when I got the call. Michaela had gone into labor and my mother-in-law was driving her to the hospital. The hospital was just over an hour away from where I worked. Instantly, my heart started pounding. We were about to meet our daughter! Then it hit me. Michaela wasn't due for another seven weeks. I didn't know much about early deliveries, but I figured seven weeks was a bit of a stretch. So I gave new meaning to the phrase *turn and burn*. I found out just how fast a Ford Escape would go.

I made the drive that should have taken me just over an hour in about forty minutes. I guess that was one perk of the job. I just phoned the officers on duty and told them not to stop me. I made it to the hospital just minutes after Michaela had arrived. They hadn't even gotten her into a room yet.

That night began the longest few weeks of my life. I'll spare you all of the medical terms and details that I would probably butcher anyway and just tell you that my wife was indeed in labor, and it was extremely too early.

They immediately started administering medication through an IV in an attempt to stop the labor. Apparently this was standard procedure. This went on for a long time. To be exact, Michaela was in labor for nine days. Yes, you read that correctly. Michaela endured nine days of labor and nine days of the doctors trying to stop said labor. For all of you who think your wife had it bad after the ten hour mark, try two hundred and sixteen hours of labor.

During those nine days I caught myself complaining that I had to sleep on an air mattress on the hospital floor. I also had a hairbrush lobbed at my head. At that point I stopped complaining. Looking back, I guess it wasn't that bad. I did go through three air mattresses. The nurses kept moving the IV pole around and it kept tearing holes in my bed. I'd go to sleep on a decently comfortable air mattress, and then I'd wake up on the cold hospital floor. I never did bill the hospital for those.

I wish I could say that the most exciting thing that happened while we were at the hospital involved a few busted air mattresses, but then there wouldn't be much of a story. Nine days after arriving at the hospital, the doctors decided that the labor wasn't stopping.

They decided it was time to give Michaela a couple of corticosteroid shots to give our daughter a better chance at not needing to be placed on oxygen. It was all quite nerve-racking really. By the time Makenzie arrived, we had a room full of doctors, nurses, and the birth team. I counted thirteen people in all. I don't make it a habit to hangout in delivery rooms, but something told me that they were preparing for something to go wrong.

I remember the doctor pulling me aside and telling me to be prepared for the birth team to take our daughter out of the room immediately to "work on her." I remember replaying those words over and over while we awaited her arrival. They weren't expecting a normal delivery. That was clear now.

Makenzie made her entrance into this world, but it was far from grand. In fact, it was unnervingly silent. She wasn't crying and she wasn't moving. Then it hit me. She wasn't breathing at all. The doctor had told me that it was normal for the baby to take short, labored breaths, but I was fairly certain that the lack of breathing wasn't a good sign.

They took Makenzie into a side room, and they told me to stay back. Two solid minutes. It was two minutes before anything happened. The doctors were performing CPR. I could hear them counting their chest compressions. They were "working on her." Two long, prayerful minutes later, I heard a cry. Then I heard more crying. This time it was mine. They allowed Michaela and me to see our daughter for a few seconds before they took her to the Neonatal Intensive Care Unit.

We didn't get a chance to hold Makenzie before they took her away. We didn't get those memories that most parents get. In fact, it was another three days before we got to hold our daughter. She spent more time with the doctors and nurses than with us for the first week of her life. Every three hours we were given the chance to see Makenzie. We were now subject to the N.I.C.U. visiting hours. They decided when we could see her. They decided where we slept, when we ate, and when we could be with our daughter. I say they decided all of that because the hospital was an hour from our home. It didn't make sense to drive home between visits. So we stayed at the hospital, ate the cafeteria food, and slept in chairs in the waiting room between visits. The visits were allowed around the clock, so at night we set our alarm clock for three hour intervals. Every three hours for seven days we saw our daughter.

We had a lot of down time between visits to think about things. During this time was when we realized that God had given us a daughter. He had heard our prayers and answered them. The doctors said that Makenzie would need oxygen for a week at the very minimum. She was never placed on oxygen. After her birth evaluation, the doctors determined that her lungs were strong enough to function on their own. Of course there were other issues. She only weighed four pounds when she came home from the hospital. The week in the N.I.C.U. was spent receiving a cycle of antibiotics along with close monitoring to make sure her body was strong enough to come home. She slept in a glass box surrounded by colorful lights and white suits, rather than in the nursery we had decorated for her. It was a long seven days on top of the first nine, but we brought our baby home on Christmas Eve. Only God could have given us a daughter for Christmas.

Chapter 4

Something Has to Give

It was a good Christmas, and it was really good to have our daughter home. She was the first granddaughter on my side of the family and the only baby on Michaela's side, so it was a really good Christmas for her too. The amount of gifts that she received was ungodly. We came close to renting out a storage unit just for her toys. I'm not sure why she needed all of those toys since she was only a few weeks old. Not only did she have enough toys to last until her fifth birthday, I was pretty sure we had everything we need to start a daycare center. I am thankful for the diapers however. Just about everyone who bought her a toy also included a box of diapers. We didn't spend a single penny on diapers for over a year. In case you don't know how many diapers a baby goes through, it's roughly a dozen a day.

It wasn't until we had Makenzie home for a few weeks that we noticed something was wrong. The problem wasn't with Makenzie. Something was wrong with Michaela. She was having trouble walking from the couch to the kitchen without becoming short of breath. At first we thought that she was just adjusting to the changes to her body and recovering from the delivery. It wasn't until she passed out that we knew something was wrong.

We made a trip to a clinic about half an hour from our house. We went to the emergency department and told the receptionist that my wife had passed out and that she was also having shortness of breath and chest pains.

Until this point I had always heard that if you're having chest pains it kind of puts you on the fast track at the emergency room. I always pictured it being like on TV, you know, they run out with a wheelchair, page the doctor, and rush you back to a room. I now know that television shows are full of lies.

We sat in the emergency room with my wife having chest pains for the next three hours. We were finally admitted and put into a little room. I'm pretty sure it was a broom closet until they ran out of beds, then they quickly turned it into a room. The doctor came in speaking broken English and asked what the matter was. After explaining the problem to him, he ran a few tests and then gave us the bad news. He declared the chest pain, shortness of breath, and fainting to simply be caused by bruising of the chest cavity. It was news to me. I've never had a bruise cause me to pass out. I wanted to argue with him, but I didn't. He was clearly a professional.

So we did the only thing we knew to do. We went back home. The shortness of breath continued, the chest pains worsened, and it wasn't long before Michaela passed out again. This time we tried a different hospital. To our surprise, we were given a different diagnosis. This time it actually made sense. This time the doctor came in, sat down, and told us that he needed to speak with us. He informed us that Michaela's test results had been sent off to be verified by a specialist. He had also made us an appointment with said specialist.

It doesn't take a genius to know that when the doctors say they need to talk with you, and that they are having your results verified, that what follows next is usually bad news. This much the TV shows had right.

He sat down, and then with a sorrowful tone, he explained to us that Michaela's heart was enlarged by eighty percent. He went on to tell us that one of her heart valves had stopped functioning as well. He then explained that there were different levels of heart valve failure, but to spare me from butchering a few more medical terms, I will just say that it was bad.

He explained to us that she most likely needed a heart valve transplant and that if she were left untreated, it could be fatal. He didn't cut corners or put spin on it. She would die if she didn't get a heart valve transplant.

If we hadn't been pushed to a breaking point with everything else, this would be sure to finish the job. We made it through the all of the scares at the hospital, the N.I.C.U., and bringing our daughter home. Now we faced a bigger giant. I can't imagine how Michaela was feeling. We had just brought our daughter home from the hospital, and now she was facing a potentially fatal heart condition. I was barely keeping it together. All the possibilities were running through my mind.

I felt responsible because I had wanted a daughter, and now the stress and trauma from the labor had caused my wife's heart to stop working properly. I realized that I might have to raise a daughter alone, and even worse, she may have to grow up without a mother. Thankfully I had a lot of vacation time saved up at the Sheriff's office. I used all of it. I took six weeks off work so that, if this was going to be it, I would at least spend it with my family.

You hear the stories on the news or social media. Maybe it's even a family member who had been given the diagnosis. I've always said a prayer for those kinds of people. I've always had sorrow for them, but it's never been so close to home. When it's your wife or your child, those feelings of sorrow and those little generic prayers don't cut it. Maybe it's because the anger gets in the way of the prayers or maybe the sorrow feels more like you're suffocating. I never thought it would be us. God was taking me on a roller coaster. There were twist and turns and dips, and I was ready to get off of it. I was sick and close to vomiting, and I just wanted it to be over.

Over the course of the next few weeks we got to know the heart specialist pretty well. We were in and out of his office weekly. Test after test, conversation after conversation, it always ended the same. They'd always say that maybe the next time something will have improved.

I've talked about church on and off and how I pray when I really need something. That had kind of been the extent of God in my life for a long time. We thanked God for Makenzie being home, and then I cursed Him for what was happening to Michaela. I went to church when things felt right. We had a pastor who I trusted. To be honest, I think I trusted his faith in God more than I actually trusted God to do something. We decided we should go to church. It was kind of a last resort for me. I wanted God to do something. He had to show up or this might be the last straw.

It'd been five weeks since our world came crashing down around us. I had one more week off, and we had one more appointment to see the Cardiologist. That Sunday we went to church and told the pastor what was going on. He prayed for us. It wasn't that intimate setting where you stand at the front of the church and say a silent prayer. Pastor told our story and then the church as a whole encircled us and prayed aloud. They prayed that God intervene and heal my wife. By the end of the prayer, the church was filled with the sounds of people crying and thanking God for hearing their prayers. We were surrounded by people who cared about us, and we hugged everyone who was there that day.

We went home in what was one of the most somber moods I'd ever experienced. It's kind of like when you finally get up the nerve to tell someone how you feel about them, and they don't reply right away. That's kind of how it felt. We had just expressed our desperation to God, our brokenness and our need to Him, and it was answered with silence. We were at the point of breaking. We were desperate, and we just needed something to give.

Later that week that appointment day arrived. We woke up, got dressed, and headed out to see the Cardiologist. We sat in the waiting room, neither of us saying much, and waited to see if God really cared about us. Another series of tests were ran, accompanied by another long wait for the results. Then the doctor came in. He was smiling. It wasn't an "I'm sorry, remorseful kind of smile" which he might have been wearing to lighten the mood. It was a different kind of smile. He seemed genuinely happy. Two things ran through my mind. Either this guy was a jerk for walking in with a smile on his face when he had even more bad news, or maybe it wasn't bad this time.

He sat down and began to explain. He said that it took him a bit longer than usual because he had to double check the results. For a moment I didn't breathe. I was trying to, but my lungs weren't listening. The doctor explained to us that Michaela's heart had not only returned to its normal size, but the heart valve had started working again. He told us that he couldn't explain it. He explained that he had been a doctor for a long time and had never seen this happen before.

After a few months of check-ups, tests, and appointments, we were told that we were in the clear. When this had all began we were told that under no circumstances were we to try and conceive another child. We were told to take all precautions to prevent that from happening; it was too dangerous. At our last appointment we were told that there wasn't any reason that we couldn't have another child. Everything that had gone wrong, and everything that had tried to break us, had just gone away. It was around this time in my life that I really believed again. I believed in the power of prayer and it was at this point that I knew He was real.

Chapter 5

The Big Move

As newlyweds, one of our big ambitions was to one day move to the mountains. I always figured it would be after I worked twenty years at the sheriff's office and retired. We honeymooned in Gatlinburg, Tennessee and if you've never been to Gatlinburg, you need to stop reading this book and go. You can finish this book sitting in a cabin with the mountains outside your door.

Okay, maybe that's not an option, but you should really add it to your "to do" list. Gatlinburg became a favorite spot of ours. We went at least once a year. We loved the mountains, the cool air, and the peacefulness of the place. We never thought that moving there would really be an option, at least not any time in the near future.

As we drove cross-country towards our new home in Virginia we had to stop in Tennessee for a day visit. That place never let us down. As we left the next morning and started our trek into Virginia we were welcomed by the Blue Ridge Mountains and the Appalachians. Tall, bluish-green peaks meeting the clear blue summer sky. As we drove deeper into the mountains, we watched the "miles to destination" counter tick down on our GPS. We didn't know until we arrived in Roanoke that we were just two miles from one of the on ramps for the Blue Ridge Parkway, and nine miles from the Appalachian Trail. The city is known as the Roanoke Valley. Roanoke sits with the Blue Ridge Mountains on one side and the Appalachians on the other side. Regardless of which way you look, you are aware of God's creation. You are aware that life is about something bigger than everything you've experienced.

The mountains in Virginia weren't that much different from Tennessee. The only things missing were the memories, but I figured it wouldn't take long to make new ones. It was surreal for a long time. Our twenty-year ambition had just come true four years into our life together. I loved my childhood, but I couldn't help but be proud that we had made the big move, and now our kids would get to grow up with the mountains in their backyard. A place that I looked forward to visiting once a year was now where our family would call home.

I'll skip all of the unpacking and settling in, and go straight to the point where the job I had just moved 924 miles for was yanked out from under me. The position with Homeland Security closed. They sent me an email. No phone call, no apology. Just an email letting me know that I was no longer being offered a job. Just in case there's a chance the guy who sent me that email is reading this book, thanks a lot buddy.

So, I reverted back to the one thing I knew how to do. I started applying for sheriff's offices, police departments, and security companies. I had an interview at a sheriff's office, but after being offered the job I learned they required a two-year contract agreement. The penalty of breaking the agreement was ten thousand dollars. I still had hope that Homeland Security would call me back, so I turned down the job.

My next interview was with an armored car service. I went to the interview, and after sitting for an hour or so learning about the job, it seemed pretty decent. So, I took the job. After a polygraph test, FBI background check, fingerprinting, and two more interviews, I was hired. Then came the firearm training, range test, armored car training course, and waiting five more weeks for my Kevlar vest to get fitted and sent to me, after which, I started the job.

I spent the next two years driving armored cars. It was actually a pretty cool job. I mean, what guy doesn't want to wear body armor, carry a gun, and drive big armored vehicles? It was kind of a guy's dream job.

I met some really awesome people during those two years. I had two great partners on the job. One of my partners had some pretty amazing stories. She left home heading straight for adventure when she was my age. She worked at Yosemite, hiked the Grand Canyon, lived in Nevada, and did some pretty amazing things throughout her life. Every day I'd spend the better part of ten hours talking with her and hearing her stories. They were all laced with adventure and uncertain outcomes, but the one thing that was the same in all the stories was that she didn't let the unknown stop her from living life. She's still a good friend even though we don't talk as much anymore. If you're reading this Michelle, thanks for the stories, and the inspiration.

I'll be honest with you, I wanted to live those kinds of stories, but the money wasn't there. By Christmas, we had two very young, very expensive kids.

We moved to Virginia with the promise of a federal income and great benefits. We rented a rather expensive apartment in the city, and with it came a hefty cost of living each month. When I ended up making half of the income I was expecting, we realized just what it meant to live on a budget. In fact, no matter how many times I entered the numbers and no matter how many times I redid the budget, we had more bills than money. This led to another bad season of our lives together. On the outside, life was really great. We lived in the mountains, had a son and a daughter, I had a cool job with a decent income, and we lived in a city that had endless amounts of things to do. On the inside we were maxing credit cards, staying up at night trying to figure out if the electricity was actually going to stay on, and praying. We did a lot of praying. Does anyone notice the pattern yet? Bad things happen and I pray. I spent a lot of my life using God as a lifeline rather than actually having a relationship with Him.

We got ourselves into more debt than I could describe to you. We owed a lot of people a lot of money. My parents would send the occasional check in the mail and I'd cash it and use it where we needed it. We'd act like it wasn't a big deal. It was a very big deal. I was a husband, a father, and a son, and I was failing at all of the above. I couldn't provide for my wife and kids, and my parents were still padding the bank account for us. I wouldn't have been able to tell this story if it were still our current situation. I have a bad case of pride. I remember when my parents were helping us. We never talked about it. We acted like if it wasn't mentioned then it wasn't happening. I'd really like to say that I woke up one day, learned how to manage money, and formulated some grand plan to get out of debt. That's not what happened. Are you ready for the big reveal? The way it actually went down wasn't so graceful. The sheriff's office showed up at my door. We owed more money to more people than I can list. Not all of them were so forgiving. I'd been court ordered to pay money I didn't have. When you can't make good on a debt and the allotted time runs out, they take you to jail. I only spent an hour in jail, but that was enough for me. We came up with a way to pay our debts off. We quit spending money, we quit doing anything we didn't have to do, and we started paying our way back out of debt. I know most of you didn't see that coming. In fact, there were only four people who knew that even happened to me. Now I guess the cat is out of the bag. There was a time in my life I wouldn't have told that story, but then I realized I had to. It's part of *my* story.

We have a choice in life. We can choose not to tell our story, or we can choose to tell it. Those are the only two options. Those of us who tell our story tend to find freedom in the words. Those who don't tell their story have the same skeletons in their closet, they just haven't made friendly with them. A story is never written to be stored away. Every life is a story. Your story has meaning, it has substance, and it has the ability to impact whoever hears it. Some of you are reading this and aren't having that intimate connection to this part, but for some of you, you feel like I'm telling your story. We are all human, we all share similar feelings, experiences, and emotions, but we will never connect until we start sharing who we are with the people around us. This is me, for everyone to see. This is who I am.

Chapter 6

Choosing To Live

I remember growing up in a modest house. I remember that a lot of the kids at school had newer things or maybe they had the more expensive brands. That was never a big deal to me, but sometimes I wondered if we weren't as well off as some of the other families. I really wasn't sure how to gauge it. We went on trips to the mountains, the beach, and to theme parks. My dad was a Master Chief in the Navy and my mom was a teacher. I didn't know much about the military or teaching, but I did know that they had to make pretty decent money. I remember my dad bought used vehicles. They weren't the kind that looks like they were ready to fall apart the moment you drove them off the lot. They were the kind that looked new, but had some mileage on them.

My parents are smart people. They are also some of the best people I know, and I'm not just saying that. A lot of my friends didn't have their dads at home. I did. Even though he was gone from time to time for work, I knew he was coming home. As a kid, it didn't bother me. In my mind he was on a Navy ship fighting terrorists. I don't think that's what he was actually doing, but it impressed my friends nonetheless. I had a mom at home who took care of my brothers and me. She made sure we didn't lack anything we needed.

She sacrificed so much for us. They both did. I had more than most people. I didn't have the newest gaming system or the most expensive brand of clothing, but I did have a mom, a dad, and everything I needed. That's not to say we didn't get a lot of stuff we wanted. We actually got most of the things we asked for.

I remember that my brothers and I always got to play sports and go to the movies. We also got to go on church trips. Looking back, I'm pretty sure my parents made good money. I just didn't understand something as a child that I understand now. It took a conversation with my dad to really get it. It was something that he said coupled with a few things that I kind of picked up on.

My dad and I were talking when I was in my early twenties. We were talking about smart choices, smart spending, and smart living. He had and still has more wisdom than I can soak up. Because of my financial situation, he was kind of coaching me a bit. He was talking about not spending more money just because you make more. Turns out my dad makes pretty good money. You couldn't tell by his lifestyle simply because he is modest. He doesn't spend a lot just because he makes a lot. When he does spend money, it's typically because he is helping someone who needs it. I remember when he bought a used motorhome. Since he bought it, he's had it in the shop multiple times. He continuously has to work on it. He could have gone out and bought a brand new motorhome, but he was content with a used one for a fraction of the price. He's actually probably spent more money working on the thing than he paid for it.

He taught me that life isn't about having the newest product, or expensive cars, or whatever it is that people are currently caught up in. He taught me that you don't have to spend money to be happy, which is something I needed to learn. My dad wasn't just showing me how to live humbly, he was teaching me how to live.

When my wife and I had children I couldn't stand the idea of hand-me-down clothes, or second-hand shopping. My kids were going to have the best, newest things. I didn't like borrowing stuff from people because it was much more fun to buy our own. Since then I've tried to lock away my prideful, arrogant side. Since then I've learned that it takes a village. I've learned that God puts people in your life to help you through life. When we turn down a gift or help from someone in our lives, we are telling God that his resources aren't sufficient.

It's kind of funny. If you believe in God and the Bible, then you have probably heard the scripture about God providing your needs (Phil. 4:19). In context, the scripture is specifically speaking to people who are living out God's will and spreading the gospel, but we tend to overlook that and wait for God to give us what we want. Even when we get it right and God does provide the resources, we often turn them away. We expect God to give us a pay raise at work when we pray for help with our finances. Instead, a friend offers to hand down some clothes to our kids, or offers to foot the bill for dinner and we say no. We tend to do this out of pride, or because we are still waiting on God. Too often we miss God when He's standing directly in front of us. We expect God to show up riding a cloud, so we miss Him when he just walks up and says, "Hey, I heard you, and I'm here."

I think about God being a person. He walks up and offers you everything you've been needing. He offers you the answers to all your questions, money for all your needs, and even some stuff you didn't ask for. The only problem is that He forgot the new car you asked for. He brought you the money you need to fix your old car, but not enough for the new one. I think If I were God, which is a stretch of the imagination, and I had just looked around and saw all your needs, went and gathered up all the resources to meet your needs, and you told me to keep walking, I might do just that. I might dump all the stuff on the next grateful person I see and call it a day. I've read enough scripture to know that God knows we are flawed. He knows we are idiots sometimes, and He loves us enough to tolerate our ignorance. In that, I find a lot of peace. I say this because I am one ignorant, flawed human being.

Chapter 7

A Foot in the Door

Sometimes we don't have to run after God to find Him. Sometimes He trips us, pins us down, and tells us to be quiet and listen. That's kind of how it happened. After moving to Virginia and finally landing a job, I figured the next thing to do was to find a church. There was a church in Roanoke that a friend recommend to us. I had heard good things about the church, so we checked it out.

The first Sunday we went to the church we were actually impressed. We met a handful of people and it seemed to be alright. It was at least worth visiting again. After a few Sundays, we got to know Russon and Nicole. Russon was the student and children's pastor, and his wife Nicole helped out with the kids. They seemed like pretty cool people. At some point Russon asked me if I'd like to help out with the youth ministry on Wednesday nights, and at first my answer was no. I liked going to church and I liked being known as a churchgoer, but I wasn't really big on the idea of volunteering. Don't get me wrong: I liked working with teens. The idea of it all sounded great; however, actually showing up on Wednesdays after a long day at work didn't sound as good.

Eventually, Russon was convincing enough and I showed up on a Wednesday. I immediately felt peace about the whole situation.

I'm not sure why God was pursuing me so relentlessly, but He was. I wasn't overly eager to serve, but He was making it clear that He wanted me there. Here comes the plot twist. After Russon had convinced me to come on Wednesday nights and help out, he told me that he and Nicole were leaving the church. It wasn't like, "Hey I may be leaving later on down the road." They were only going to be there for one more week. Luckily, we had become pretty good friends and we all stayed in contact. We actually became even better friends after they left the church.

Here's the thing. The longer I helped out at the church, I started to notice things. I started to see behind the scenes. Things weren't adding up. Another youth leader was brought onboard to lead on Wednesdays, and I continued to help out. She was really good at the job and she cared about the students. Sadly, as things went on, I started to notice a lack of commitment from the leadership. I believe that they had good intentions, but it seemed like regardless of how hard we tried, things never got done. We needed things for Wednesday nights, but we never got them. We didn't have a budget, and when we asked for supplies for the youth room it seemed more like pulling teeth. It's not that I think that they didn't care about the church or the people there, but something was wrong. No matter how hard we tried, things never happened the way we planned. It seemed like there was always a problem needing to be fixed.

This was roughly a year after Russon and Nicole left. I started to have my own opinions on things, and that didn't go over very well. I started to see the church more clearly. There were a few people who made the decisions and that was it. If you didn't follow suit then you were no longer needed. I quickly became worthless to them. I won't tell someone else's story, but my friend also found herself in the same situation. She's no longer at the church either. There was a pivotal point for me during my time at that church. Actually, I guess there were few.

It's kind of funny how God can use a body, a building, or really anything he wants in order to accomplish His will. This church was in no way a place we felt that we could stay as a family, but it did give me nearly two years of experience volunteering with students. My family also grew to include Russon, Nicole, and their family.

Also during my time at the church I got to attend a youth camp with the students. It was in North Carolina. It was an amazing weekend. I think it was there that I knew my calling was to ministry. This guy named Jonge Tate was speaking, and there was something he said that stuck with me and I couldn't shake it. He was teaching out of the book of Romans and he hit on Romans chapter 9, verse 17. The scripture talks about how God raises us up to fulfill His purpose. I took that scripture home with me. I didn't have paper so I actually jotted it down on the back of my hand in red ink, and I spent the rest of the weekend praying about it. The crazy thing is what happened next.

I was online later that week looking at ways to start up a website and trying to figure out how much it would cost. Michaela asked what I was doing. While I was at camp that weekend she felt God calling her to start some kind of website. It was random and she didn't understand it. After we talked, we realized it was confirmation for what God had called me to do. That night we launched Romans917.com. We've done a lot of different things with the website, but mostly you can find free devotions that my wife and I, along with a half-dozen other writers post each week.

Earlier I talked about going to writing school and how it had been a waste of time. I think it would have been a waste of time if I hadn't decided to devote my life to ministry and to God's purpose for my life. With Him it wasn't a waste, it was preparation for His plan. When I was taking writing classes I never would have guessed it would have been so that I could write free devotions on a website.

I always thought of myself as a songwriter, or an author. If you're reading this book, then at least God humored me on the latter.

I told you that my wife confirmed that I was on the right track with starting a website and writing devotions. That part is true, but the confirmation I got a few months later is going to blow your mind. It's going to be the part of the story that makes you stop and wonder if you've missed anything in your own life. Maybe God is trying to show you something as well.

It will be kind of like watching a good court case, or cop drama. You're waiting for the case to come together. You're waiting for the prosecutor to present that one piece of evidence that is irrefutable. Once it's presented the case is over. That's the kind of thing that I'm talking about here. I'm going to wait a bit before the big reveal. After all the things that went on, the church camp, the disappointment, and the new friendships, it was clear that I had managed to get a foot in the door to ministry.

Chapter 8

Getting In My Way

You know those stories on the news or online about communities coming together to help out a family who suffered a tragedy? I really like those stories. They give me a little bit of hope. Sadly, it's often just the opposite. Normally when you turn on the news or even social media you see all of the bad in the world. Whether it's a suicide bomber overseas, a missing child, or some big box store kicked a homeless man off their property because the homeless guy was making the customers uncomfortable, there's always tragedy in the world. I know that the last example seems directed. That's because it is. I remember hearing about that happening multiple times this past year on the news. A homeless man who is simply seeking a warm place to lie down ends up making some self-righteous customer feel uncomfortable. It really makes me sick. If I have to explain why it makes me sick then there's really no reason for you to finish this chapter.

That's the problem with society. Jesus wouldn't have told a homeless man to find a different bench to sleep on. Sometimes I like to picture Jesus the way He was, as a man, rather than as God. I do this because as a man, I can relate to Him a little bit better. I think if Jesus were here and saw the way we treat people He would probably slap us in the back of the head and tell us to wake up.

This is the problem with the whole idea of God. We keep God locked in a box up in the sky, miles away, and we never think about the fact that He walked this earth just like we do now. The only difference is that he got it right. I like to relate myself to Jesus as a man. I often re-live situations or just picture something that is going on with Jesus standing there, looking on like the rest of us. Every time I do this He always does something. He inserts Himself into the situation and makes some kind of impact. Then, I think about the fact that we are supposed to live like He lived. We are supposed to imitate Christ. And when I realize that I didn't step in and help like Jesus did, I start feeling pretty lousy. My train of thought takes a sharp turn and I start thinking of all the things that I'm still not getting right and I start a pity party in my head. A lot of times this party continues into the night and I drift off to sleep making promises to God, to Jesus, and to myself to do it differently the next day.

That's another problem I have and I seriously doubt it's just me. If you don't have the same problem, then please share your secret with me. I like to make lists and set goals for myself. I don't just make daily checklists or set career goals. I set goals in every area of my life. I set spiritual goals, goals at work, and goals with my family, and so on. The problem is that I start measuring my character and value by whether or not I reach my goals. I wake up and give myself a pep talk. I'm not going to lie today, not even those white lies that slip out from time to time. I'm not going to have road-rage. I'm not going to spend too much time in front of the computer screen writing, and I'm not going to neglect my family.

I'm also one of those "all or nothing" kind of guys. By the time I get my socks on my feet in the morning, I've already screwed something up. I mark the day off as a loss and start making those same promises again. Maybe tomorrow I will make it until lunch without screwing up. This becomes dangerous when we start setting goals in our relationship with God. He really wants it to be a relationship but we make it a task. We figure if we can keep from doing that one sin that tends to pull us down, then we can count it as a good day. I no longer think this way. I now realize that God doesn't want to be on our "to-do" list. He wants to walk with us. He wants to love us, and He wants us to love Him. I think a lot of this comes back to the fact that as a society and as a species, we love ourselves too much.

Setting goals makes me feel good. Achieving goals makes me feel awesome. Making my relationship with God a checklist gives me a goal to reach and something I can succeed at. My relationship with God is based on what I want out of it, and not what He did for me. We are extremely selfish people. In fact, most of what keeps us from God simply comes back to us loving ourselves too much.

Road-rage is something I deal with from time to time. It prevents me from loving people the way I should. It keeps me from loving people like Jesus loves them. When a car cuts me off I immediately don't love them, at least not at the moment. The reason I don't love them is because they just added a solid ten seconds to my commute home. Those insensitive jerks. Those stupid people who can't drive. I mean, it's ten seconds. I am more concerned with what time I will get home than what time they will get home.

This would be one of those situations where I mentally insert Jesus. I picture Him getting cut off and it never fails, He remains cool-headed. He really does love us that much. As much as I hate realizing how deeply rooted my love of self is, I love being reminded how deeply rooted His love is for us.

It really doesn't matter which of my many flaws I bring up. Regardless of the problem, it most likely originates from the fact that I keep letting myself get in my own way.

Chapter 9

Street Dogs

My buddy Patrick recently returned from Peru. He was telling me about all the places he went and the things that he experienced during his couple of weeks down there. He showed me a great deal of amazing pictures. The pictures had a kind of simplicity that only God could create and still make overwhelmingly beautiful. He had a ridiculous amount of pictures of cats and dogs. The dogs were street dogs. I had heard of places around the world that were overrun by street dogs, but I had never actually seen it until now.

One picture stuck out more than the others. He showed me a dog that was sitting on a welcome mat outside a nice looking shop. The dog was peering in through the perfectly polished glass doors, but you could tell that he knew he couldn't actually go in. The people were going on about their business. I couldn't tell anything else about the scene from the picture, but I imagined the people inside casually looking out and making comments about the dog, but nobody moved to offer him food or to let him inside. He was a street dog. They knew his place, as did he.

Sadly, this made me think of the church. I think the church tends to see people who don't live the "Christian" lifestyle, as street dogs. Maybe it's because of an image, a lifestyle decision, or maybe because of their past, but regardless of the reason, they're street dogs. I think if we allowed more street dogs to come inside we might find them to be much less of a street dog and much more like us.

I've visited a lot of churches in my life, and I've called only a couple of them home. It's sad, but I haven't seen too many that actually demonstrate the love of Christ the way Christ did. I know that sounds like an ignorant statement, because of course Christ loved like Himself, but isn't that what we are all supposed to be doing? Aren't we all supposed to love the outcasts and the nobodies? And I use those terms lightly, because in God eyes there's no such thing as a "nobody." We all have value, but sadly, Sunday service is the one place that instead of giving value to all people we tend to place a price tag on them the moment they walk through the doors. The people who are righteous, or at least self-righteous, tend to get the bigger price tags, while all of the street dogs are deemed worthless. We want them out as quickly as possible. That's assuming they were even able to walk through the doors in the first place.

I think it has a lot to do with political correctness which sickness me deeply. I think Jesus would close the door on most churches in the country simply because we look nothing like the church He had in mind. Jesus wasn't big on politics. He was a real person who really loved people. He loved *all* people. Yes, despite the self-righteous doctrine that is typically preached in America, Jesus did, and still does, love the homosexuals, the murderers, and the guy with all the tattoos. He loves them just as much as the widows, the children, and the guys who are *actually* teaching His Word.

I worked at a church one time that was so caught up in public image that I'm not even sure they still knew what it meant to love people and to serve. The service projects happened around holidays and in big public places where they would be seen. For those service projects, the price tag wasn't really an issue. On the flip side, when it was time to go into the neighborhoods that really needed outreach and get our hands dirty, we seemed to not have the money. I don't think it was really a money issue. I think it was because we didn't have an audience. The church was more worried about whether or not it looked like a church than actually being The Church that is described in scripture.

I've always heard people say that they don't attend church because they've been burned by the people in the church. I don't think that's a very good excuse, but I will say that I believe them. I've seen dead churches. I've seen pastors who preach the word but never live it. I've seen pastors who use their position of authority to gain power and favor in their communities. I've heard pastors cast judgment on people in a church and talk about them behind their backs. If there is anything that can kill a church quickly, it's gossip. I never knew that until I experienced it.

Paul was clear on how dangerous it is to have dissension inside the church (1 Corinthians 1:10). He explained how we are all one in Christ and that we should live in community and harmony with one another. If you want to break up leadership teams and destroy a church from the inside out, all you have to do is start talking about the members of the church. Start gossiping about the leadership, and then lie to their face when they call you on it. I know it sounds crazy. It sounds like a bad soap opera, but it happens. I've seen it.

If we are ever going to love people the way Christ did, we've got to stop focusing on marketing God like He's a product. Church has become like a bad infomercial. Whichever preacher sells it the best has the bigger church. God isn't a product and I'm sure He's tired of us treating Him like one.

Churches like to have big buildings with big signs that say something clever on them in an attempt to pull people in. We like to have big pews with big stages and big speakers. We like big gyms for the students and lots of food to get the kids interested in God. In my opinion, if a church can't afford to go out and feed their community, then they shouldn't be buying million-dollar buildings. If you can't spend a couple hundred dollars to help a family in need, don't spend a couple hundred thousand to build a new gym. The problem with these churches is that feeding a family in their home doesn't give off the impression of being Christ-like, not that it isn't. The problem is that no one is holding up a sign that says, "Hey, look what we're doing". If it doesn't bring the spotlight down on the church, then it's not enhancing the image of the church. We avoid doing things that Christ would have done in order to keep up an image of being a proactive church. It's such a twisted concept.

The bottom line is that political correctness is going to be the death of the church. And it's not like there aren't churches out there who are actually making a difference, but the "look at me" Christians are making it extremely hard for actual followers of Christ to accomplish the last commandment Jesus gave us. He told us to go and make disciples, but instead people are seeing past the smoke and mirrors and seeing the hypocrisy for what it is. When people start associating the church with hypocrisy and fake people, then it becomes extremely difficult to share the love of Christ with them.

This is one of the reasons some of you will be offended by this book. It's not exactly politically correct. I'm not going to sugarcoat anything that I believe is worth saying. I'm not going to act like what the church is doing, or at least the majority of the churches throughout our country are doing, is okay. It's kind of ironic that we have churches that have hundreds of people, and some churches with tens of thousands of people that attended weekly, but no real impact is being made. I'm not trying to discredit the organizations and churches that are making a difference, but if everyone who went to church and claimed to follow Christ actually did, then the world would look differently. There are over three hundred million people in the United States. Over one hundred million claim Christianity as their religion. I simply refuse to believe that if those one hundred million Christians were actually living for God that our world would look like it does. If the Christian church fails anytime soon, it won't be due to a lack of opportunity, or resources. It won't be because the world isn't getting a chance to hear the Word and respond to it. It will be because of the political correctness and hypocrisy within the church.

Chapter 10

Full Circle

After leaving the first church that I worked at in Roanoke, I was set on finding another one to call home. I knew that if I got in the habit of not going to church on Sunday, then I might fall back into the same old routines that kept separation between God and my family. Russon and Nicole had found a church they really liked soon after leaving the first church. They had been attending for about a year when we started looking. They invited us to check out the church. Russon and Nicole had started volunteering at the church with the students and helping out with odd jobs that needed to be done. That's one of the things I admire about the two of them. They are always serving the church. They're always serving *as* the church.

So, Easter Sunday was around the corner and we decided to go check out the church Russon and Nicole were going to. After attending the church for just one Sunday we knew that there was something much different about this church than any we had been to. The people were genuine. They weren't putting on a show or trying to play church. They were real people who were hungry for the Word. They were like a family. There wasn't dissension and there weren't different groups of people within the church. They were one body who were carrying out a common goal. They were being *the* church.

We sat there in our seats waiting to get our first glimpse at the pastor who we would listen to for the next hour. The music started to play and after a couple of worship songs the pastor walked out onto the stage. The pastor of the church was Jonge Tate. You may remember that name from earlier when I was telling you about a church camp I had went to at my last church. He was the guy who had spoken in such a way and with such conviction that it led to my family and me launching an online ministry. Jonge was the reason that I fully committed to ministry. He was the one who had spoken so powerfully that I knew that I had a bigger purpose than self. We went a few more times to the church before deciding to make it our home. Russon introduced me to the student ministry pastor and his wife. The very next Wednesday I started working with the students. Everything had come full circle.

This church was doing it right. They were loving people, serving people, and keeping each other accountable. It's a beautiful thing when God's people actually live out His purpose for the church. It also makes it clear that most churches in the United States aren't getting it right. This church was deeply rooted in the teachings of Christ. They were active on a weekly basis in missions and outreach, and they truly demonstrated the meaning of being servants of Christ.

At one time in my life I was studying psychology, not because I cared about psychology, but because I knew I could make a lot of money telling people what their problems are. One of my favorite things that I studied during that time was the *bystander effect*.

The bystander effect is a theory where something bad happens to someone. Let's say you are at a restaurant and someone has a heart attack. They are helpless, but there are dozens of other people in the room. You stand there doing nothing. You don't call EMS, and you don't perform CPR. You do nothing. They say the reason behind this is that you believe that someone else will do what needs to be done. You figure that out of all the people in the room, someone else is already calling for help. You figure that someone else will save this guy's life.

This is a huge problem in the church. We expect the missionaries to go and offer aid overseas, the pastors to reach the lost in our community, and the Sunday school teachers to make sure we know what we need to know. The problem is that in a church of a couple hundred people, this leaves over eighty percent of the church doing nothing. We not only neglect the spiritual health of the people around us and around the world, but we neglect our own spiritual health. We leave it up to other people to make sure we are sound in our faith.

Jesus' last commandment before leaving this world was for us to go out and make disciples. He was speaking to a select group of people, but the implications carry over to anyone who carries His name. We are all missionaries. We should all be ministers to the people around us, and we should be making sure our own spiritual health is maintained. All of these things are the reason that we are still at our new church. Put simply, it's because they are actually being The Church.

You know, I guess I kind of learned what serving other people is about from a book I read. I'm sure that you've noticed I learn the most when I read. I like reading. I think someone famous once said that reading is the gateway to knowledge. I'd tell you who it was that said that, but I don't tend to read classic novels and educational books. I like reading books about real people who have the ability to keep me entertained. The book that I read is called *10 Days Without* and it's by a friend of mine, Daniel Ryan Day. If you haven't read it then I encourage you to pick up a copy as soon as you finish mine.

In his book, Daniel talks about all of these things that he went ten days without having. He picked things that we often take for granted. He went ten days without shoes, using his legs, and I think he went without a jacket during the heart of winter among other things. It was really inspirational. It made me wonder what it would be like to go without things I used on a daily basis. I literally read his entire book in one sitting. That was on a Saturday. Sunday morning I got dressed and headed to church with the family. Well, I didn't get completely dressed. I had decided that for the next ten days I wouldn't wear shoes. It was December and it was forty-six degrees that morning. I distinctly remember how cold it was because my toe had just enough time to become numb before I ran it full speed into the curb in our parking lot. The pain was still very present, but I think the winter air had numbed my feet enough that my eyes didn't tear up.

I went ten days without shoes in an effort to raise awareness for the millions of kids around the world without shoes. Yes, I said millions. I did a little research and was absolutely blown away by the statistics I found. Twenty-one thousand children die every single day because they don't have shoes. Their feet get torn up from walking around barefooted. The infection sets in, and they die.

I found an organization that could provide a simple pair of shoes for a child for a one dollar donation. So I set my goal. I wanted to raise one hundred dollars over the ten day period. I would walk into a public place barefoot while ice was falling outside, and people would immediately take notice. Most of them walked by while staring at my feet. The money started coming in when people started becoming too curious to just walk by. They had to ask why I wasn't wearing shoes. I figured that the people who didn't ask me probably just assumed that I didn't have any shoes and they didn't want to make me feel bad. Every time someone asked why I was barefoot, I simply explained what I was doing and I asked for a one dollar donation.

During those ten days, my feet bled three different times. After having my feet numbed by the winter weather all day, jumping into a hot shower didn't feel as good as you'd expect. The numbness went away and the pain set in. I slept with a pillow under my feet every night just to get a little relief. I didn't take any painkillers either. The kids over in Africa can't grab painkillers and I wasn't going to either.

On day ten I had collected just shy of twelve hundred dollars. I also stepped on a nail on day ten. I almost made it the full ten days without a trip to the hospital, but not quite. It actually took a few days for it to sink in. It all started with reading a book and then deciding to do something that was bigger than myself. Through this I had been able to supply over a thousand children with a pair of shoes. That's the moment I realized just how easy it was to make a difference in the world. You don't have to have a big plan, or an army behind you. You just have to decide that it's time to do something.

Chapter 11

Camping With the Enemy

I remember this camping trip that a bunch of my friends and I planned our junior year of high school. There were about half a dozen of us who were going to wait until the temperature dropped and then go hang out in the woods doing guy stuff. We'd sit around the campfire, talk about girls, and dare each other to do stupid things. And of course, we would do all of the stupid things we were dared to do because we were guys. We had reputations to uphold. We couldn't be seen as real men if we chickened out at a campout. We went to one of those small town schools where everyone knew what happened over the weekend by the end of first period on Monday.

It was around March. The temperature was still pretty moderate, and it was a bit on the cold side at night. We picked a Friday and we all met up at a buddy's house. We went deep into the woods, found a good spot to start a fire, and started what quickly became a very bad camping trip.

There was a surprise waiting for us at the camping area. What we didn't know was that one of the guys who came to the campout had planned ahead and hidden a case of beer in the woods. There was an unspoken awkwardness most of the night. Most of the guys there felt uncomfortable with the whole situation, but none of us wanted to be *that* guy so we just kind of all went along with it.

My buddy, Jon, came to that campout, and looking back I am glad that he did. At the time we were pretty good friends. He was a better person than I was. I went to church and tried to stay on the right side of things, but he was really into the Bible. He led Bible studies and quoted scripture. He even did that kind of stuff at school. I figured it was some kind of social suicide, but he never thought twice about it. He was always the voice of reason anytime we did anything.

Later that night I decided to have a beer. Another friend of mine had already had a few too many, and I figured one couldn't hurt. Looking back, it did hurt. In fact it hurt my ankle. After having too many beers, my buddy jumped on his four-wheeler. I hadn't had much to drink, but for some reason I still decided to get on the back of the four-wheeler with him. We were in the woods and it was early in the morning, I think around two or so, and for some reason I thought this would be a good idea. We would just go on a joy ride.

The entire ride lasted less than five minutes. That's all the time it took for my buddy to ask me if I thought we could make it between two trees. I said no. He tried it anyway. A few seconds later, my foot was pinned between the four-wheeler and the tree. I was facing forward and my foot was facing the opposite direction.

After we panicked for a few minutes, we decided to go up to his house and I would sleep it off. We figured that I could go to the hospital in the morning without getting in any kind of trouble for drinking. That is where Jon came into the story. My buddy and I were just hanging out at his house when we heard his parent's bedroom door open. Jon, being the voice of reason and being concerned for my ankle, went and woke my buddy's parents. After a very drama filled hour or two, which included a fight, I went home. My ankle was indeed pretty jacked up.

You don't realize the value of a situation until it's over, at least not very often. I went to school on crutches that Monday and the moment I saw Jon I took a swing at him with the crutch. I wasn't mad because he had been the voice of reason, because truthfully he really was trying to look out for me. I was mad because I had gotten in trouble. The reason I had gotten in trouble was a direct result of my own actions. He knew it would make him unpopular, but he did what was right. That's the reason I like having people like Jon in my life. Sometimes you need someone who will be self-sacrificing to look out for you.

A few years later Jon and I had patched up our friendship. In fact, I had the honor of being the Best Man in his wedding. Jon still lives in Louisiana, so we haven't gotten to really catch up in a few years, but we still have our friendship. We don't talk that much on the phone anymore, but when things get real for either one of us, the phone normally rings. It's good to have a friend that you can count on even after months of not making time to talk.

I think about God that way sometimes. Even though God is available to us daily and He walks with us, we treat Him like a friend that lives a thousand miles away. I don't promote going long stints of time without talking to God, but the awesome thing about God is that He isn't going to change how he feels about us, and His love isn't going to change due to a dry season in our lives. Sometimes I wish Jon and I talked more, but I know that if we met up for coffee tomorrow, it would be as if nothing had ever changed.

It really doesn't matter how far you feel from God or how long it's been since you picked up the phone so to speak. God is still there, He still loves you, and He still wants to talk. Our relationship with God was never intended to be a long distance relationship. It was designed to be intimate and often.

I think more often than not, intimacy gets left out of our relationship with God altogether. I remember as a child I would just tell God what I was thinking or how I felt. I remember thanking Him for my food and actually meaning it. It wasn't a ritual back then. God really was my father. He still is, but I think we forget that sometimes. Maybe we've been going to churches too long, the ones where the prayers are drawn out and precise. No prayer is complete without theological jargon that puts emphasis on our knowledge of scripture. I really get irritated at those kinds of churches. It's a stage production and nothing more. It's like we can impress God with our performance and how well we know a script that we wrote for ourselves.

God wants to be intimate with us. He wants us to come to Him crying when we are hurting. We don't need to use words every time we pray. God hears our hearts. That means He knows what we are feeling, what we want to say when words fail us, and He knows what we need. So to think that we can put on a show for God or perform and gain something by it is ridiculous. God sees past the smoke and mirrors. He just wants you. He wants me. He wants us to love Him and He wants to love us.

Chapter 12

It Takes a Village

I learned the value of people when I was in my early twenties. I learned that there aren't too many things in life worth doing if you have to do them alone. Really think about that. Whether it's been a vacation, a life-changing experience, or an achievement, would it have been the same if you had to experience it alone? I can't think of a single experience that would have been the same if I had been doing it alone.

As a side note, I've also learned that if you don't have the right people with you in life, then it's the same as not having anyone at all. It may even be worse. I think about trips I've taken with my family. I love turning to them and seeing the looks on their faces when they experience different things for the first time. I love sharing life with them.

We've got to make sure we don't just have spectators in our lives. Instead, we need people who are going to hold us up when life gets tough and cheer us on when we finally get it right.

I remember when I was moving from one job to the next, one church to the next. We had just started our ministry and we were moving to a new house. Everything in our lives was new. That's a scary place to be. One of the things that gets us through change is still having a constant to lean on. We were literally changing all of the things that gave us security within the span of one month. This is when I knew I had good people in my corner. This is when I knew we'd be okay.

We received a card from Russon and Nicole. It was simple, but it meant the world. They just wanted to let us know that we did in fact have people in our corner, and they believed we were making the right decisions. Ultimately, they just wanted us to know they were here for us. They wanted us to know that we didn't have to go through all of the changes alone.

I have heard an old saying many times in my life. You know the one I'm talking about. *It takes a village.* I had a basic understanding of the saying, but now it had personal relevance. I realized that we had found our village. We moved nearly a thousand miles from what we knew as home. We had experienced trial and change on a frequent basis, and we had questioned the entire thing a few times. What kept us going was the fact that we had people who were willing to tell us that we'd be okay and they had our backs.

Our lease was coming to an end at our apartment complex and we still hadn't found a place to live yet, at least not a place we could afford. I had just changed jobs and when you write that you've been working at a new job for less than a month on a housing application, people tend to demand a bigger deposit before they'll hand over the key. I joked about living in Russon and Nicole's basement. At least it started out as a joke. We cut it close, but it didn't come to that. Just knowing that they would have allowed us to live in their basement made me realize something. They weren't just friends; they had become family.

I sometimes joke with Russon about him being old. The truth is he's just a few years older than me, but I like to mess with him about it. Sometimes I call him an old man, but he's really more like a big brother. We've got a lot in common, I'm just slightly better looking, depending on who is telling the story.

It's evident all throughout scripture. We were never meant to live a life of social isolation. The church isn't just a meeting place for God's people to hang out; it's so much more than that. The church was designed by God so that His people could do this thing called life together. In order for us to act as the body of Christ, we have to be pretty involved in each other's lives. It takes unity, and that's exactly what God wants for us. He wants us to come together as a community.

One of my favorite examples of what it looks like to live as a community is found in the book of Acts. In Acts chapter 2, verse 40-50 we get a pretty good idea of what the church is supposed to look like.

In this story, people where listening to the gospel being taught and they were devoting their lives to the teachings. Thousands of people were being saved. My favorite part of this story is that it doesn't end there. It goes on to talk about how the people were coming together as a community and selling their possessions and distributing the things and their money to anyone who had needs. It says that the people received their food with humble hearts and praised God for it. Because of this, God added to their numbers daily those who were being saved.

Salvation was never meant to be the final step. We preach the gospel as if the *sinner's prayer* is the ultimate take away. That prayer is actually never even mentioned in the Bible. That's just man's way of interfering with the way things should be. Salvation is the first step in living for Christ. As the people in the story accepted salvation, they were moved to sell their possessions and help those around them. They demonstrated the simplest meaning of community. Because of this, God continued to add to the church. This brings me back to unhealthy churches. Ever wonder why churches fail to grow and prosper? It's probably because they aren't really the church at all. They aren't being faithful with what God has made available to them, so they just sit stagnant and decay. The truth is that without community any church will eventually die. It really does take a village in the truest sense of the word.

Chapter 13

Sex and Roses

When we are young, I think we all have different views on how relationships are supposed to be. We have different views on friendship, dating, and marriage. I think our views on relationships often stems from the relationships that are on display around us.

I grew up seeing my parents get along pretty well. They married young, and they are growing old together. If you were to ask me what it means to be married or stay married, I'd say that once you make the decision, it's for life. That's the example I saw growing up.

If you ask someone who came from a divorced home or maybe someone who saw his or her parents dating one person after the next, then you might get a different kind of answer. Children who grow up seeing abuse, cheating, and neglect often assume that this behavior is normal in a relationship. I work with teens every day who have distorted views on every aspect of life. If you were to ask some of them if physical abuse is okay in a relationship, they'd say yes. They'd answer this way because it's what they know. It's what they've always seen around them.

For me, I grew up in the church. Growing up in a Southern Baptist church has its downsides just like any other upbringing. Talking about sex with regards to marriage was a rare occurrence, and any mention of it outside of marriage was strictly forbidden. As I got older and started dating Michaela, I started to gain a better understand of what it meant to be in a relationship. I wasn't good at it yet. It actually took me the entire dating relationship and part of our marriage to really start getting it. It's a lot more complicated than people tell you when you are attending premarital counseling. It's not that it's harder, it's just different. The main thing that makes marriage difficult is that most of us enter into this sacred relationship with little to no concept of what it means.

I didn't know a lot going into marriage, but I had watched a lot of movies, television shows, and read a few books that did incorporate the topic to some degree. I figured that this would help me transition into marriage. I was terribly wrong. It was the movies and shows and the books that gave me the most problems.

I really have grown to hate the way Hollywood portrays love, relationships, and marriage. It's nothing like the real thing. You see, it turns out that Mr. Right isn't really as sweet or romantic as the shows want you to believe. I know, it's a crazy thought, but it's true. I know a guy who does screenwriting. Those guys in those romantic movies are actually just actors reading from a script that has been doctored line by line. It blew my mind when I first learned this too. Those roses are actually props. He didn't really buy them for her, the prop guy did. And for that girl to look like an *All American Sweetheart,* it took hours of makeup artists' working their magic. She practiced those lines over and over until she was able to say them in a believable way. And I'm pretty sure she doesn't like sex as much as they are making it out. It's all a big scam.

The problem is that these movies set the standards impossibly high and the real world won't let us live up to them. They don't write the petty fights and bad moods into the storyline. They don't include the misunderstandings and forgetfulness that normally lead to those petty fights and bad moods. They only include the good stuff and when we buy into this idea of relationships we make it so that our partner can never match up. If you want those kinds of scripted moments then you should become an actor.

I learned that marriage is about so much more than any of this. Marriage is about learning what the other person doesn't like, and avoiding those things. It's about becoming best friends, and going through tough times together. It's about making memories, not the cheesy scripted kind, but ones that real people experience.

I'm not saying that marriage doesn't need romance and its own level of cheesiness. It does. I still like the fact that my wife puts notes in my lunchbox for me to find when I get to work. I like opening my lunchbox in front of my co-workers and making a show of reading the notes at the table so everyone knows I have an awesome wife at home. I love when Michaela posts something cheesy on social media and tags me in it. It lets me know that she doesn't just love me, but she loves me and wants everyone to know it. It's kind of like staking claim of me, and I think it's hot.

I like it when I get a text message from Michaela asking if I can come home early because she misses me. And yes, that might be why we keep having kids at such a quick pace, but I don't plan on changing a thing.

I remember going on a church trip while Michaela and I were still dating. She couldn't go on the trip, so it meant that we'd be away from each other for a solid week. When you are a teenager and you are used to seeing someone almost daily, a week seems like forever. We talked every night on the phone, but it just wasn't enough.

At the end of the week everyone who went on the church trip went out on the town before we headed back. Michaela and I had been waiting all week for that night because she had arranged to meet me downtown. I'll never forget seeing her running across the parking lot, and the hug that followed. It was a good feeling. It's one of the moments that I realized that what we have is real. It's one of the moments that real people experience. And the best part about was that none of it was scripted. If the love is real, it doesn't take props and scripts to make the moments you have together special. It simply takes having those moments together.

Another one of my favorite memories was our honeymoon, and not just for the reason that you'd expect. However, we did save sex for after the wedding, so that was great too. We went to Gatlinburg, Tennessee. We had a little cabin along the river, and it was snowing. It was awesome! One of my favorite memories was the fireplace, but not because it was cozy. It was one of my favorite memories because we couldn't figure out how to set the thermostat on it. It was a gas log fireplace, and we had no idea how to work it. I thought I set the thermostat to seventy two degrees. It turns out I didn't. We woke up in the middle of the night with a huge puddle of sweat in the bed. The thermostat wasn't set on seventy two, it was set on ninety. We slept the rest of the night with the patio door open because we never did figure out how to set the temperature. It stayed on ninety, and the door stayed open.

It isn't the trips that go perfectly that we remember. It's the unexpected things that stick with us. It's the things that catch us totally off guard that make an impression. I've always been the type to try and give my family the best things in life. I try to take them on a certain number of trips each year. I want to make memories so badly that sometimes it seems forced. It's a bad habit. I spend so much time planning things because I feel like if I'm in complete control then I can make them go the way I want them to. Most of the time this has the opposite effect. It takes the fun out of it.

It's taken me the better part of ten years to learn these things. It's taken me that long to stop trying to make every memory perfect. I've learned to enjoy them as they come. This includes marriage. If you spend your entire life trying to perfect your marriage, or trying to make it match up to something you've seen on a movie, then you will never be satisfied. You will always be reaching for something that you cannot obtain.

Again, I'm not trying to persuade people to give less than their all to the relationships in their lives. I believe that when we do anything, that we should give it all we have. There is a difference between giving it all we have and trying to make it something that it was never meant to be. God is pretty clear on marriage. He's clear on the importance of resolving issues the day they happen, and that sex is important for having kids and maintaining accountability within the marriage. He's clear on the man's role to lead and to protect, and that his partner should be supportive and loving. You can get the basis for a good marriage and for a Godly marriage from the Bible. Beyond that, the rest is up to you. Your marriage will be what you make it, but it will also be what you allow it to be.

Marriage is ultimately about becoming the best of friends, learning to work together for a common goal, and living out life together. It's about deciding what you want to do together, and figuring out your strengths and weaknesses. It's about making up for your partner's shortcomings, and it's about letting them make up for yours. It's about learning to live with the fact that your partner isn't perfect. It's about not giving them a standard to live up to and more about just letting them be themselves. Marriage is about a lot of other things too that I'm probably forgetting to list. But I do know this; marriage is not just about the sex and roses.

Chapter 14

Cup-a-day Christians

I was standing in line waiting for my coffee one day when a thought occurred. You see, earlier this year I was at a leadership conference where some of my favorite speakers were going to be teaching on the principles of leadership. During intermission there were dozens of tables set up in the lobby promoting different organizations. Among these tables was an organization that had opened up a coffee shop downtown. They had gone over to Africa and saw the poverty and living conditions. They were there because they wanted to make a difference. They wanted to make a real impact in the world.

After brainstorming a bit, they decided that they could teach the people a trade of some sort that could lead to jobs and better standards of living. It turns out that the soil along with the climate created a perfect setting for coffee plants to flourish. This led to the birth of an organization, and now a coffee shop. The people grow the beans, which are then shipped to Virginia and sold in a coffee shop. They had created a foundation for jobs and growth in what once was an impoverished area of the world. On top of that, they have now drawn attention to a real problem. You can buy shirts, mugs, and bumper stickers along with the coffee, and the proceeds go to supporting these people. They had accomplished something bigger than themselves.

Of course, being at a leadership conference where they were teaching about being a solution to the problems in the world, I got inspired. There was a problem and I wanted to be a part of the solution. Now before you start thinking too much of me, know that I really didn't do anything that amazing. I had normally stopped by this little retro coffee shop on my way to work where I paid way too much for a half decent cup of coffee. So, in a stroke of genius, I knew what I had to do. I switched coffee shops. This is the coffee shop where I now stand in line every morning waiting on my coffee. The prices are actually better, but because of their cause I normally include a tip. I'm not really saving any money, but I feel like I'm making a difference.

So, like I said, I was standing there in line when I had an epiphany. And since epiphanies don't happen to average people, this just confirmed my new found status as a genius. Okay, not really, but I did realize something that made a lot of sense. Most of us are simply cup-a-day Christians. I'm not implying that every Christian drinks coffee, though something must be wrong if you don't. I'm saying that we have that mentality that I developed at the conference. I know it's sad that at a leadership conference I had decided to do something that I thought was noble but turned out to just be normal. We do something like buying a cup of coffee because of who's selling it, rather than actually getting out there and really making a difference. I had convinced myself that I deserved a pat on the back because I now paid two bucks a day for coffee that some poor people were growing. My coffee habit was keeping people alive in Africa. I hope you sense the sarcasm in that statement.

And I then realized that it's really selfish in itself. Instead of donating to the organization, which would have made a bigger impact, I was only willing to give if I received my coffee in return.

I wasn't going to go by the coffee shop and give them two bucks without getting my coffee. I had successfully turned an opportunity to impact someone else's life into something that was really more about making sure I had coffee in the morning.

A friend of mine once jokingly asked if buying coffee from an organization like that could count as tithe. Part of me wanted to say yes, and part of me wasn't sure. I still don't have an answer, but I do know that if our heart isn't set on really making a difference in people's lives, then it's basically pointless to give in the first place. And if we are giving out of compassion and love then we probably wouldn't mind giving the extra money outside of what we would normally give.

I realized that the one thing that got in my way more than anything else was me. I can look back, and it's sad but, I benefited in some way every time I had given to someone. Sometimes it wasn't a cup of coffee or financial gain, but simply the fact that I got to feel good about myself for a day.

Really think about it. When was the last time that you went out of your way to make a difference in someone's life and you got nothing in return? When we write a check to an organization we typically write it off on our taxes. When we buy a product that supports a good cause, we still end up with a product and sometimes it really is just for the ego boost.

I have a confession to make. I really like titles. I like being known as someone. Unfortunately, in school I was the fat kid, or the kid that took geometry too many times. I'm not as overweight as I used to be and I know my shapes now, but I still think about those labels sometimes. Maybe it's because of all the bad labels I've had that I tend to find security in the titles I hold.

I have a tendency to doctor my resume when I'm applying for a new job. It's amazing the difference that little words can make on a resume. I'd search for bigger words that meant the same thing to interchange with my actual job title. I worked at a sign shop when I was a teenager. All I did was assemble boxes and package campaign signs into them to be shipped out. If you read my job title on my resume you would have thought I was some kind of prodigy. I think I finally decided on "Sign-Pressing Supervisor" as the title on my resume. You know, because that's a thing.

Sometimes I jump at opportunities to serve because I get to wear a name tag. Not literally, but I carry the title. I become important for the moment. I worked as a Community Outreach Coordinator, and no joke, that was my title. Sometimes it took a lot of phone calls and planning to make the outreaches happen. It was a headache more often than not, but I did it. I went to meetings after getting off work late, stayed over after the services were over on Sundays, and stayed up all night at youth group lock-ins because it gave me some kind of purpose.

I don't remotely regret doing all of those things even though they were somewhat selfish. People were still impacted, and some even came to know Jesus. I just wish that I had it in me to be genuinely compassionate all of the time. I wish I was the kind of guy to come up with a plan that would change the world, and then actually follow through. I've planned a lot of things. This is the third book I've attempted to write. The planning is fun, or at least thinking about the planning is fun. Then I realize that the plan actually takes time and effort, and it becomes a headache. Typically, this is where I scratch the plan and start trying to think up something else. If I did half of the things I've thought about doing, I'd probably win some type of medal or something.

My point is that most of the time we have good intentions as Christians, but we let ourselves get in the way. We settle for doing little things that makes us feel good about ourselves instead of flying to Africa and building a coffee plantation. I want to be a coffee plantation-a-day Christian rather than a cup-a-day Christian.

Chapter 15

Finding Favor

Sometimes we have to have something happen to us personally before we can truly understand it. Sometimes faith only comes from undeniable encounters with things we can't explain. I've always read the stories in the Bible where God gave His people favor, or maybe He showed up in a way that was unexplainable by any other definition than divine intervention.

I was tired of driving armored vehicles, and to be honest, I was tired of working for a company that didn't really care about their employees. It was a corporate job with corporate mindsets. I knew that most of my job experience was limited to law enforcement types of jobs, and my education was geared toward music and writing. On the flip side, I had been working with students in the church youth group for a couple of years and I had those seven months as a preschool teacher under my belt. I figured this was a decent foundation and with that in mind I decided to start looking for another job.

I spent the next few months hopping from one job search website to the next without any real luck. Finally, I came across the website for the Virginia Baptist Children's Home. They were looking for counselors to work with the at risk teens in their residential programs. After reading the job requirements page, I was quite certain that I didn't meet any of the requirements, but being desperate, I applied for a job anyway.

I was counting on my volunteer work with the youth group to meet the experience requirement, and I was hoping that my music education would meet the college requirement. I had no idea how a music and writing education would hold any real merit at the Children's Home, but I was really needing some kind of change, so I figured sending in my resume couldn't hurt.

I remember sitting there staring at the computer screen. I was reading and then re-reading a message that said I had successfully completed the online application process. I remember sitting there and asking God to please give me favor.

In the past when I had applied for a job I always followed up with a phone call to make sure the employer knew I was serious about the job. This time was different. I told God that I was leaving it in His hands, and that if He wanted me to have the job then I would get it. I shut down the computer and went to bed. I'd like to say that I left it in God's hands because I have lots of faith in Him, but it was mostly because I didn't think I met any of the requirements and if I didn't get the job I could just use God as an excuse.

Regardless of the reason, I kept my word. I didn't follow up on the job. I really didn't think about it after that night. Submitting the application was more of a way for me to feel like I was at least trying to change my circumstances than anything else.

A few weeks went by and I was driving home from work one Friday evening. I was drained and aggravated and ready to throw the towel in. As usual, the day didn't go the way I had planned, and I was now driving home after a thirteen-hour shift. The only real relief I felt was knowing that it was now the weekend. That's when my phone rang. I was in bumper-to-bumper traffic in downtown Roanoke, and I didn't recognize the number. I started to let the call go to voicemail, but my curiosity got the best of me. I answered the call, and to my surprise, the Director of the Children's Home was on the other end of the line. He didn't waste any time getting to the point. They had reviewed my resume and felt that I was qualified for a position they currently had open. They set up an interview for Monday morning. The only catch was that the position was at a residential camp about an hour drive away from Roanoke, in New Castle, Virginia. All of the positions in Salem had already been filled. Salem was only nine miles from our apartment. New Castle was two counties away.

I figured that even with the long drive that it would still be a new job. It would be the change I was looking for. I agreed to the interview and spent the whole weekend resisting the urge to type a resignation letter for my current job. I figured that if I typed a resignation and didn't get the new job that I would still be tempted to quit anyway.

That Monday morning I started the hour drive over Price Mountain and down into New Castle. The views were breathtaking. I figured if I did get the job the views alone would make the hour drive worth it. In addition, the road that led into New Castle provided bird's eye views of the Blue Ridge Mountains.

As I turned onto the road that led into the camp I was surprised that it was an actual camp. As I drove down the gravel road leading into camp, my car immediately developed a grey tint and a nice coating of dust on the windshield. On one side of the road stood a gym and cafeteria that looked a bit outdated, and on the other side stood a bathhouse and well-shed. Right next to the bathhouse stood a bunkhouse and a trailer that held a dozen canoes. They were hunter green with *Old Towne* painted along the side like a work of art. At the end of the road sat a building with a parking area and a covered porch. It looked newer and a little more business-like than the rest of the buildings. It was the administration building, or as they called it, the staff lodge. This is where I was greeted by the Director of the camp.

For the next hour I sat listening to details of the job and answering questions about why I wanted the position. At the end of the hour the Director stood to his feet and extended his hand to shake mine. He was offering me the job. He told me I could go home and think about it for a few days but I declined his offer and immediately accepted the job. Change was in reach, and I jumped at it. It turns out that my time working with the church youth group wasn't considered because I didn't have any documentation to support it, but my job at the preschool actually gave me what I needed as far as requirements go.

I went straight home and typed up my resignation. Well, I typed it after I took the family out to eat and celebrate the new position. With every keystroke came a bit of freedom. I didn't wait even a day to turn in my resignation. I arrived at work the next morning a few minutes early, marched up to my supervisor's office, and put the resignation letter on his door. I smiled a little bit more each day I drove away from that place simply because I knew I was a day closer to leaving for good.

It turns out that I should've waited a couple of weeks before turning in my resignation, but looking back I definitely don't regret it. The hiring process at the Children's Home was extensive. So extensive that it took eight weeks from my interview until my first day on the job.

At first I viewed this as a big problem, mainly because we were broke and my income had just been placed on hold. One of the guys I met during training and orientation was Adam West. He's the Senior Director of the residential programs at the Children's Home. That makes him my boss. I actually met him at a Casting Crowns concert that the Children's Home had given my family free tickets to. I met him because it turns out we were sitting in his family's seats instead of our own. Looking back, I'm glad it happened that way.

We talked a bit, and he was aware that my background checks were taking longer than the usual six weeks to clear. I was sitting at home stressing about not having any income when the phone rang. It was Adam, and he wanted to know if I'd like to come help him out with some stuff around campus. I was hesitant at first, but then he told me that I'd get paid as long as I was doing something and then I was all in. I didn't know it at the time, but it was the second bit of favor God had shown me. The first was when I received a job offer for a job that I wasn't truly qualified for.

Adam found enough training and odd jobs around campus to keep me busy until my background checks finally cleared. He extended compassion to a complete stranger. I was just another employee, one who had taken his seat at a concert, but for some reason he wanted to help me out. Later he told me that it was at that concert that he felt a connection to me. He said that he was watching me hold my son and worship God and that there was something special about seeing that. It meant a lot to me then, as it still does. It was the start of a friendship that I deeply value.

Another reason Adam played, and still plays, such a vital role in my story is he's a man who allows God to use him for His purpose. Adam has favor from God, and he extends it to the people around him. Luckily, I get to be a part of that inner circle.

There are lots of ways that God showed me favor over the next couple of months. Remember when I said that we were broke? I wasn't just saying that for dramatic effect. It was a struggle to put gas in the car just to get to work each week. It turns out, as beautiful as the drive to New Castle was, it was also extremely expensive. I found myself spending over four hundred dollars a month just to go to work and back. I remember one Thursday evening I was driving home and thinking about the fact that I didn't have enough gas money to get to work the next day. Payday was a couple of days out, and we were out of money. That's when the phone rang. The caller ID was flashing "Adam West" across the screen. He had a project that he needed to finish that Friday, and wanted to know if I'd come down to Salem and help him out with it. You see, I didn't have enough gas to get to New Castle, but I could definitely make the nine-mile trek to Salem.

It took everything I had to keep my composure until I hung up the phone. Then for the next few miles I cried, and I prayed. I thanked God for seeing my needs and meeting them. This happened a total of three times. I was out of money and praying, and the phone rang. Every time it was Adam asking me to meet him in Salem. One time he even picked me up from my house without me asking. He didn't know that God was using him to answer my prayers. That's what's amazing about God. All we have to do is open ourselves up to His will and love people. He does the rest.

All of this was during that time in my life that I finally figured out how to manage money. I had already made the necessary changes and now we were on the slow climb back to financial security.

For a long time I was one of those guys who had trouble having faith. I'd hear the stories about miracles and how God saved the day but I still harbored doubt. Sometimes it has to happen to us to make it real. Sometimes we have to see the face of God before we can truly live like He exists. I see the face of God through the little things in my life.

You would think that with all that had happened with Michaela and with our daughter that I would have developed an unshakable faith. For me, I just need to see Him in the little things. If I can see that He cares about whether or not I have gas money to get to work, then I know He cares about the bigger stuff too. We all experience the love of God in different ways. We all have languages that we understand better than others. Some of us need encouragement or affirmation. Some of us might need an answered prayer, and still for some of us it's something else.

For me it's simply having a need and seeing it met. I imagine this is because I've always been horrible with money and resources. So to know that God sees my stupidity and still loves me enough to reach out one more time brings a type of comfort that is unexplainable.

Chapter 16

Just Be Something

I distinctly remember someone telling me that I can't be everything to everybody. It was when my family and I branched out to start our online ministry. They didn't even pull me to the side and tell me. Instead they posted it on my social media wall for everyone to read. They called me misguided. This was because I wanted to help as many people as possible, and to that person, this wasn't realistic. The problem was that I had limited experience and resources. I had never ran an organization, let alone started one. I expected the people around us to rally and support us. Instead, I received a public slap in the face. I'll never forget that day. I'll never forget those words.

At the time I didn't have a response. As badly as I wanted to argue and call them out the way they had called me out, I didn't know what to say. I'm glad that I didn't have a response at the time. Now I've had time to cool off. I found the answer later on down the road.

When we launched our ministry I wanted to help with every issue under the sun. After learning the cost to run a ministry capable of doing that, I decided to take the time to sit down and really decided where we wanted to make a difference. Jesus commanded us to share the gospel to all nations, so I knew whatever it was needed to have global impact. This is when it hit me. I knew how to write, and I knew how to start a website. We launched the website as an online resource. We decided to start off by writing devotions and offering them for free on our website. Along with this, we did fundraising and we sent the money to organizations that already had established themselves. We knew that they could use the money for whatever was needed. I did some research and contacted a few online campaign companies. We were able to get our website featured in ads and campaigns to get more traffic to our website.

We have the ability to track the number of people who visit the website and read our devotions. We can also keep up with the countries and even the states that the online traffic originates in. By the end of the first six months we had successfully taken the gospel, through our devotions, to over forty-five countries. To date, we have presented the gospel to nearly a half a million people. We average a hundred or so views a day. It's not a lot compared to other websites, but it's reaching people. If I compare the daily number our website reaches to how many people I was sharing the gospel with in person, then I had added about a hundred people a day to that number. So, basically I wasn't really sharing the gospel like I should have been.

It really bothers me when Christians become lazy. We sit on the pew so long that it practically attaches itself to us. We weren't made to fill pews. We were made to be active. If you don't try to make a difference, then you won't make a difference. For most of us, what we are able to accomplish comes down to the perspective we have. Believing you can do something is the hardest part sometimes, but God promises us success. As long as we are doing His will, He will give us the resources needed to move forward. Since His will is for us to share the gospel and to love people, then I can say with confidence that we can be successful. God also tells us not to fear (Isaiah 41:10). Fear is a lack of faith in God. It's like telling God that our fear is bigger than He is. I have fears, but I'm not brave enough to tell God that my fears are bigger than he is. He made me, and he can unmake me. So this means my only option is to have faith.

The problem with pew-fillers is that you can only focus on a thing or two at a time and still be successful. If you are so focused on filling the pews and keeping your numbers up, then you most likely aren't sending people out. And a church that isn't sending people out on missions is a church that isn't doing the will of God. A church that isn't doing God's will isn't a church at all. At that point, we are simply a group of people occupying a building.

Most churches today preach messages that will guarantee that people will come back. They preach "feel good" messages. They are willing to sacrifice integrity for the sake of popularity.

I've never liked going to my boss's office and being told all of the things that I am doing wrong. More so, I've never liked being told that I need to change something. Humans aren't designed to accept criticism and correction easily. It's our sin nature that prevents us from being receptive to this. So, when we go to church and the sermon makes us realize something is wrong in our own lives, then we don't necessarily want to go back the next Sunday. Most of us, by the time Sunday gets here, have already had a long week. The last thing we want is to go and be judged by other people and then feel like we need to change our lives around. So to maintain the numbers and the checks rolling in each month, we're teaching what sells. If you can go somewhere and be told you are great and that you are doing everything right, then you are likely to go back. Let's face it, we all like having our ego stroked.

So like I said, at first I really didn't have a rebuttal for the guy who publicly slammed me. After my head cleared and I started down the new road I had chosen, I started to really reflect on it. It played in my head almost daily because I was worried that he might be right. I was worried that I would have to apologize for getting angry. We can't be everything to everyone. There's no way around that. It's just not possible, not because we can't be good to people, but because we won't get the chance to be everything to everyone in this lifetime. However, we can be something to everyone we meet. We can listen to people who need to be heard, we can love the hurting, and we can feed the hungry. We can be Christ in some way to everyone we encounter.

I also remember a couple of other things that were said to me at the time. A friend told me that I was jumping in too quickly, and another guy told me that ministry wasn't easy. He told me that I didn't know what I was getting into. Again, I really didn't have a response at the time to either one of these things. Now, I guess I'd say that I didn't jump in *too* quickly. Things actually worked out well for our ministry. I did jump in quickly, but if I were still waiting to feel things out then a lot of lives wouldn't have been impacted. Also, I haven't found ministry difficult. I think that it's difficult when you are trying to do things your own way. Maybe when you are too worried about public image, the road becomes a little rocky. It can be difficult when you are working with people that aren't on the same page as you. It's difficult when you are trying to envision things with people who don't have vision at all. The only difficult thing I've had to do so far is find time for all the things that God is doing in my life. So I guess if you ask me, I'd say jump in and just be something to someone.

Chapter 17

Status Quo

A friend and I were getting ready to head off on a two day kayaking trip down the Shenandoah River. We checked our gear, cleaned up the two-man kayak, and headed north into the Shenandoah Valley. My friend had convinced me that he was actually pretty good at kayaking. I had been a few times, but I was far from an expert. I figured with the two of us that we could figure it out and have a successful trip. After a few hours in the car climbing over one peak and back down another, we arrived in the Shenandoah State Park. We offloaded our gear, made sure it was watertight, and launched the kayak into the water.

The first few hours of the trip went well. We were winding our way through the Shenandoah Valley and taking in the beauty of the wildlife along the bank. We had brought along a couple of fishing rods, and we were actually doing well since neither of us spent a lot of time fishing. The water was crystal clear and you could see the fish weaving in and out of the rock shelters under the water. On one side of us sat trees and wildlife, and on the other we were face to face with a large rock wall that seem to reach to the heavens. It was a surreal experience. Another hour went by and the setting took a bit of a change. Instead of being able to hear the birds singing their songs and the occasional splash of a fish on the surface of the water, we now were overwhelmed by the roar of the white water that set just ahead. It was at this very moment that things took an unexpected twist.

My buddy looked over at me with a concerned look on his face. I figured this was because we weren't expecting white water so soon into the trip, but it was more than that. He tried to put together a sentence, but his nerves were causing his words to come out in a twisted mess. I started to think something might be seriously wrong. He finally managed to spit the words out. He had never actually been kayaking. He had told me that he had been because he wanted to come along on the trip with me. He wanted me to think that he was good at kayaking.

By the time his words had really settled in, we were just a few yards from the whitecaps and the drop that would surely be the end of our kayak. We didn't have time to argue or to come up with an escape plan. Our kayak dropped over the first dip in the river and the front of the kayak slammed angrily into the rocks. A few more hard slams and a mouth full of water later we were upside down under the kayak. All of our gear, the compass, and our cell phones were now lost somewhere in the white waters of the Shenandoah River.

I fought my way out of my seat and out from under the kayak just in time to see his head pop up from the water. In just the few seconds this took place we had been pushed a solid thirty yards from the kayak. Luckily for us, it had gotten caught between a couple of rocks and we were able to make our way back to it. After we flipped the kayak, walked it through the water, and climbed back into it, we had time to let everything sink in. We were soaked, still had a day and a half of kayaking, and half of our gear was now floating just below the surface downstream. I lost my cell phone and my car keys. He lost a pair of sunglasses and some other gear. He was upset because the sunglasses he lost cost a hundred and twenty dollars. I was angry for completely different reasons. My buddy had just put our lives in danger all for the sake of image.

After the trip, everything was okay. However, for the rest of the time on that trip I had a hard time forgiving my friend. It was so stupid to risk so much for something so trivial.

Sadly, I have to admit that I've done the same thing so many times in my life. I've always been a bit of an image guy. I remember the day I left the sheriff's office. I thought I should buy myself a going away present. Since I had just gotten my pension check in the mail, I went and bought a three hundred dollar wristwatch. It was my way of telling people I was successful without having to actually say it. I don't really know why I thought I was successful since at the time I was unemployed. That's just the kind of thing that guys tend to do. I won't speak for the entire male population, but I tend to find comfort in name brands and titles. I know I've mentioned that before, but it's really crazy how much we are willing to risk to maintain an image.

I see people driving around in their luxury cars that cost more than the average house in America. I wonder what motivated them to spend that kind of money on a machine that will break down just as quickly as any other. And on top of that, it will cost more to fix because of the make and model. I don't think I've ever seen someone driving one of those cars with a smile on their face. They all look worn out and beat down. They look like they hate life. They also cast their judgmental glances at my twelve year old SUV that has a couple dozen bumper stickers on the back. They aren't aware that my car is paid off, and that those bumper stickers mean I've been places. I just assume that their lack of bumper stickers means they can't travel because they are too busy paying for their car. That may not be true, but it makes me feel better about their judgmental glances.

It took me a long time to learn that brand names, fast cars, and lying about what I'm good at doesn't make me any better than anyone else. The things that define our worth are how we live, and who we live for. I've never liked the idea that everyone is a winner. People can choose to not be winners. They can choose to live a bad story. The people who are living bad stories are the people that think a fancy car will make their story better. It's not going to happen. A good story comes from living a life that makes a difference. A good story comes from experiences that cause pivot points in your life. So in a way, the kayaking trip was a pivot point for me. I realized that my friend's desire to maintain an image almost resulted in my head being smashed against the cliff face. Since then I've stopped trying to live up to the status quo. I've stopped letting things and images define who I am. Instead, I now let the story I'm telling define me.

Chapter 18

Don't Stop Dreaming

I mentioned earlier that I had a couple of people in my life that had been less than supportive when I decided to actually pursue my dreams. After being told that I was diving in too deep and too fast and being told that I'd fail, it feels good to know that those things were not true. I've always been a bit of a dreamer. I find myself arriving at work most mornings not remembering any of the road between my house and work. It's because I tend to get lost in my dream world. I know that doesn't sound safe, and it probably isn't, but neither is being limited to the here and now. Maybe I'll try and save my daydreaming for safer places than the road, but I don't know what my life would look like if I didn't spend a great deal of time dreaming.

If I didn't dream then I also wouldn't have the ability to write. Writers depend on their dreams to fuel their work. The truth is that life is too boring the majority of the time. If you want to live an exciting life it takes effort. It takes dreaming up new realities and making them happen. I look at all of the things in my life that truly matter, and none of them would be real if I hadn't first dreamed about them.

As a kid I daydreamed about getting married and having a wife. I daydreamed as a newlywed about having kids someday. Once I became a dad, I then daydreamed about giving my kids a life they could enjoy. This led to working harder and being more intentional in the things I was doing to ensure that they could have that kind of life. I dreamed about writing this book for years. Even as I write this book I am dreaming about book signings and big royalty checks. Oh yeah, and about making a difference with my story. I know that should probably have been the first thing on the list, but I want to be honest with you. I don't want you to think I'm something I'm not. Writing isn't an easy task, but there are enough benefits to keep me motivated. I really do want to make a difference in the world and I know God wants me to tell my story, but royalty checks don't hurt.

After my first trip to Gatlinburg, Tennessee, I caught myself daydreaming about moving my family there one day. We missed our target by roughly four hundred miles, but the things that had drawn us to Gatlinburg aren't so different than Roanoke. It was that little gas station right outside of Gatlinburg. You could see the street lamps that pointed you downtown. We pulled into Gatlinburg early in the morning and stopped to get gas. As I stood at the pump, I watched the mountains reveal themselves as the morning fog slowly climbed back over the peaks. There was a gentle mist falling from dark grey clouds, and if the temperature had dropped a few more degrees it would have been snow. I climbed back into our SUV and the heat slapped me in the face and thawed my hands out. It was at that moment that I knew I wanted to move our family to the mountains.

We have the ability to make any dream a reality. It all comes back to writing our story. The move across the country to Virginia didn't look easy. We didn't have everything mapped out, and to be honest, the plans that we did have ended up falling through. Almost everything that we planned failed for the first year we lived in Virginia. We had money issues, jobs fell through, and we almost had to move into a friend's basement. The truth is that if you want to live a good story then you are going to have to take risks. Not every risk is going to pay off the way you'd like. Sometimes the only pay off we get from taking a risk is that we learn some important life lesson from it. And then there are the times that things do work out. There's the moment that the doctor tells you the answer is no, and nine months later you are holding your newborn son or daughter. There are the times that you start a ministry without any money and then you get a check for several hundred dollars in the mail from a complete stranger; and yes, that happened. My point is that we have all been in that moment. Whether it's sitting on the shore watching the sunset, or pumping gas into your car while staring at the fog roll over the mountains, there is a point when it hits you. You might not know what it is, but you know it's there. It's that feeling that there's something bigger out there, and you want to be a part of it. You want to experience something more. It's what inspired you to dream in the first place. Maybe you used to be a dreamer, but you feel like it's too late to start dreaming again. Unless you are dead, you can still dream. It doesn't matter how many plans fail and how many risks come back to haunt me, I've learned that you can never let the dream die.

Chapter 19

Love of a Father

It was after becoming a dad that I learned the kind of love God has for us. My kids have to be disciplined daily, but they've never done anything that would cause me to walk away. It was while I was thinking about how much I love my kids that the truth hit me. This is the kind of love God has for us. It brings me comfort to know this.

It's actually kind of dangerous for a screw-up like me to know that God loves us too much to walk away. I have to be careful not to use it like a "get out of jail free" card. But I really do believe it's true. God isn't going to give up on us. If He were even thinking about walking away, then He would have left me a long time ago.

My concern is for the people who walk in sin and never look back. It's dangerous to accept salvation and allow our lifestyles to remain unchanged. We are given freewill. Even if we knew God as children, if we walk away from Him as adults then how can we still have a relationship with Him? I'm afraid that so many people are going to be surprised when that day comes. They are going to still be relying on some prayer they said as a kid to have locked in their salvation. The book of 1 John makes it clear that if we are walking in darkness but claim we have fellowship with God, then we are liars. It even goes as far as to clarify that we are deceiving ourselves by thinking we have a relationship with God while we walk in sin.

For me, life is a daily struggle to do what is right. It's a struggle just to get to the end of the day without feeling like a total screw-up. I think this is why the Bible tells us to put on the armor of God every day (Ephesians 6:11). We need to be ready to combat our flesh nature. You can tell which days we aren't really focused on living for Christ. When we let our guard down our flesh wins, and normally I lay in bed those nights and pray until I fall asleep. I'm normally pleading with God to let me wake up one more time and give it another shot.

After realizing the kind of love God has for us, I pray a little differently. God sees my heart. I know this because the Bible told me so. I'm not resisting the urge to break out into song. When my kids get on my last nerve and then crawl up into my lap and hug me, all of the frustration melts away. I almost forget why I was even upset with them. I'm happy to see that they are trying to make things right. That's what matters to me. My kids can be little monsters sometimes, but at the end of the day nothing changes the love I have for them. The only thing that would really hurt me would be if they walked away and never came back to their daddy. I think this is also what would hurt God the most. He doesn't need us at all really, but his indescribable love for us causes Him to long for us the way a man longs for his bride.

One of the scariest moments in my life happened just after a heavy snow. In a few hours time, over two feet of snow had fallen. I knew I'd have to go to work the next morning and our car was completely snowed in. We hadn't been living in Virginia too long and I had neglected to purchase a snow shovel. With the snow still coming down, I went outside with a three gallon trash can and started scooping snow. After a couple of hours of digging, the snow started coming down harder. It was nearly whiteout conditions. I went inside to thaw out and wait out the storm. A few hours later we had an additional couple of feet of snow on the ground. Michaela bundled the kids up and we all went outside to play around and I thought I'd take another shot at digging the car out.

The car was parked about thirty yards from our front door. I spent half an hour shoveling snow again. Then, I got in the car to try and drive it out of the parking spot. I glanced over at Michaela and the kids playing and took a short breather, and then I climbed in the car and cranked it. As I slammed the gas pedal to the floor, the car gently rocked forward, then I put it in reverse and it rocked back. I figured that if I did that enough times then I could get the car out without shoveling any more snow. I slammed the car into drive, gave it gas, and it shot forward about a foot or two. Then, as I slid the car into reverse, I heard Michaela yelling at me. When I had climbed behind the wheel of the car, she and the kids were back near our front door. I looked in the rearview mirror to see Michaela on the ground, in tears, yelling for me to stop. I threw the car in park, jumped out and surveyed the situation. Makenzie had somehow made her way over to the car, and was playing in the snow about a foot behind the right back tire. If I had hit the gas I would have ran over my daughter. With the car still running and the door wide open, I ran over and picked Makenzie up and just sat in the snow holding her. I carried her inside and sat on the couch with her for another half hour. We were all crying. Elijah was just staring at us. He had no idea what had just happened. After I gained my composure I went back outside to cut the car off.

That's one of those moments that change you. It's was a pivot point. I could have lost my daughter by a simple mistake. Suddenly all of the stupid things she had done and all of the times she didn't listen didn't matter anymore. I didn't want to let her out of my sight from that point forward. It was in that moment when I almost lost my daughter that I realized what love really was. True love is something that can't be replaced by anything else. That's why God's love for us is so important. We can walk away from Him and deny His love, but we will never find anything that fills that space like God can. It's not because there aren't good things in this world. It's because that space in our life was only meant to be filled by God, so nothing else is going to work.

Chapter 20

Church Planting

I've always liked the idea of church planting, at least the imagery painted by the stories in the Bible. Paul's missionary trips always resulted in communities turning to follow Christ. I never thought I would plant a church or even be a part of something like that. In my mind, church planting always took place in remote villages on the other side of the ocean. I loved when missionaries would come and speak at our church. They'd tell us all about the churches they had built, and how the people were so receptive of the gospel. I always liked listening to the stories but I knew that I was never going to be called to go overseas and plant a church.

Honestly all I knew was that I didn't want to put forth the effort needed to do something like that, so I assumed that it was never anything I'd ever do. I figured God knew I was a bit too lazy for something like that, so that's why He has other people to do it.

My family and I had been going to the new church for a while now, but there's something I neglected to mention. Before we ever walked through the doors of the church, Russon had asked if we could meet for lunch and talk about a few things. He knew that we were looking for a new place to call home and his family and mine had already become really close.

Before my family and I moved to a little town outside of Roanoke, Russon and Nicole had moved there with their son. They helped us find a house that was a two minute walk from their house so we could live in the same neighborhood. None of this happened by chance. I met up with Russon for lunch that day and we discussed church, family, and life in general. He asked me what my ambitions were and what I was hoping to accomplish with ministry among other things. After we talked for a while and our food had gotten cold, he told me that he and his family had actually moved to the new neighborhood to start a life group that would hopefully grow into a church later on down the road. He told me that he really wanted his family and mine to do life together and wanted to know if we'd be on board with helping out with the life group. He asked me this while we were still living in Roanoke, but it was only a few months after that when the house on their street went up for rent, and we knew that it was an opportunity to really commit to the cause.

Sometimes I can take weeks to pray about something and depending on the commitment level it would require I take even more time than that. Then there are those times that when something happens and you know that it is God. You get a peace that makes you feel overwhelmingly good. This was one of those times, so I said yes.

I know I said that I wasn't a church planting kind of guy, but this didn't require me to go overseas or leave the comforts of my home really, so I was in. A friend of mine who does missions work has always told me that it's actually easier to share the gospel overseas because the people are desperate for something. They don't have the things that we have, so they aren't caught up in constant conflict between things and God. When they are offered a chance to know God they are excited and eager. Since moving and starting up our life group, I've seen this to be true. It's not like I am out every day canvasing the neighborhoods, but I have invited people to the life group. I've given them the run down on what we are doing, and most of them have better things to do on Sunday evenings. It's currently the month of September, and right now that *thing* would be watching football games.

With that said, the life group is going well. We've been meeting in the basement of Russon and Nicole's house. It turns out to be a good thing that we didn't live in their basement because then we would be having church in our bedroom and that would be weird. The only time that I question our decision to not live in their basement is when it's time to pay rent each month, but most days I am glad we didn't move in with them.

Even though I didn't like the idea of how much a mission trip would cost, I've always liked the idea of going overseas and helping people. I think part of that comes back to feeling important. I don't do it on purpose, but I tend to hold the guys that go overseas up a little higher than the ones who do local missions. I mean nothing against the local guys. Everyone needs love, community, and to know Christ. People can't be two places at one time. The mission of the church can only be completed when you have people dedicated to every field of missions. There have to be people overseas and in our local communities living on missions every day. The funny thing is that I always thought we would at least get to choose were we did our ministry. I figured that God was pretty laid back and if we committed to ministry that he would let us choose when and where. It turns out that if we really want to do His will, then we will go and serve where He wants us. For me and my family, that place happens to be a small town in Virginia. Don't get me wrong; I believe that God still lets us write our own story. He directs the story and sometimes sets the scene for us, but it is still up to us to write the story.

David Gates

When we were living in that small town in Louisiana I would never have guessed that we would move to Virginia, go through a crazy series of events that would lead to ministry, and then move one more time so that we could help plant a church. The cool part is that I didn't have to know what was going on for God to fulfill his plan in my life. We get may get gut-feelings, or nudges, or whatever you want to call them, but we all know when God is speaking to us. He speaks in different ways. The best thing we can do is pick up a pen, and be ready and willing to go where he wants us. We have to listen to those little voices of reason that speak to us so regularly.

Chapter 21
Not For Sell

I've always been really into reading quotes. Sometimes when I'm bored I can spend hours looking through quotes online. I do this for the same reason I love to read. I can gain a plethora of knowledge from things that other people have figured out. John Quincy Adams once said, "If your actions inspire others to dream more, learn more, do more, and become more, you are a leader." I really like this quote. I think that any real leader has to live up to these standards.

I've learned that it is extremely easy to be a supervisor or a boss. It's easy to tell people what to do and delegate responsibility. A true leader has to be capable of doing so much more than that. A real leader should be able to capture the room when they begin to speak, not because of their position or title, but because they have proven themselves to be valuable and a great teacher. There are only a few people that I tend to hang on their every word. That sounds kind of cheesy, but there are a few people that I've met that have earned that kind of value in my eyes.

My dad is one of those people that doesn't have to ask for respect in my book. He demonstrates fairness, love, and integrity with everything that he does. He's a leader when no one else is willing to step up. He goes above and beyond for the people around him, and for that I credit him as a true leader.

Most of the clichés are true as well. Real leaders really do lead. That means always putting the team first and working for the good of the people you are leading. It means first in and last out. You've got to be willing to be the first to hit the clock in the morning and you need to be willing to stay until its closing time.

President Truman had a sign that sat on his desk in the White House. It said, "The buck stops here." You've probably heard of passing the buck. It means passing the responsibility. President Truman didn't believe in finding a fall guy when things went wrong. For him, the buck stopped with him. He would take responsibility for himself, the people around him, and for whatever went wrong. For that reason, I respect him.

A real leader lives by this motto. As a Lieutenant at the sheriff's office, I had the opportunity to lead a team. I had a couple dozen officers who relied on me to make the right calls. Unfortunately, I was young and still had a lot to learn about leadership back then, so I made a number of mistakes. Even with my blunders, I think you could get a collective answer from my team if you asked them to describe me as a leader. I took care of my team. I had their back, and in return I knew that they had mine.

I believe that we are all called to be leaders in a sense. We might not all hold positions of leadership inside the church or at work, but we are all leaders in a way. As a husband and a dad, I am responsible for leading my family. It's my hope that each day I do what's best for my family and keep their interest ahead of my own. When I go to work I get the opportunity to be a leader to teens who have never seen what a leader looks like. I hope that I am setting an example for them that lives in their memories as they become leaders themselves.

Mothers have a responsibility to lead their kids and to teach them what it means to have integrity and character. Children, especially older siblings, have a responsibility to lead their brothers or sisters, or maybe their peers at school. I'd be willing to bet that somewhere in your life you are seen as a leader. You may not even know who it is that sees you that way, but you have to be mindful of the fact that someone is looking up to you to be an example in their life.

I get kind of heated when I think about politics and how things have changed over history. A seat in office used to be won over by good men. Integrity, honesty, and a sense of morality was required if you wanted to obtain a position of authority and leadership. Now elected officials are typically decided by who can spend the most money on their campaign or, sadly, who can buy the seat. At one time we had men and women leading this country that had something to offer. They had good intentions and ethics. Now it's more of a money game.

I have a problem with leaders who could be bought at a price. I've known people that would take bribes to maintain power, or even worse at times, they'd turn a blind eye to maintain their status and position. It's easy for most of us to think that we'd never do something like that, but the truth is that a lot of us do it without paying any attention to it. When we know that something wrong is going on, we have a responsibility to say something. Most of the time we sit by and do nothing. Whether it's because of fear of losing our jobs or because of our social status, it's wrong. Evil runs amuck in this world because we'd rather play it safe than stand up and make a difference.

Especially as the church, we have to take our role as leaders seriously. I don't necessarily mean inside of the church building as much as to the outside world. We are called to be the salt and light of the world, but I think most of us have let the flame burn out. If we aren't leading and standing up for what's right, then what are we doing? The majority of unchurched people still look to religion for answers. I'm not sure why that is, but when bad things happen in the world they tend to look towards the church for a response. If we aren't willing to step up and lead then what kind of message are we sending people? Could it be because we claim to want to help people that they look to us, or maybe it's because we are supposed to be making a difference and we talk about it all of the time. So, when we fail as leaders we end up looking like a bunch of liars instead. Maybe this is where the church gets a bad reputation.

As leaders we have to start exhibiting integrity, honesty, and true leadership qualities. We've got to stop looking the other way and letting evil win. We've got to stop exchanging our values for personal gain. Leaders shouldn't be defined by power or wealth. The measure of a leader really does come down to whether or not they are inspiring people to be more, do more, learn more, and dream more.

Chapter 22

It's Really Going to Happen

I've had some friends who have gone through their midlife crisis. They'd go out and buy a motorcycle, get a new haircut, or whatever it is that makes them feel young again. I even know one couple who decided to have another kid. Now they have a toddler walking around while their other kids are off to college.

Looking in from the outside, I never really understood the concept. Lately, for some unknown reason, I've started to understand what they went through. I'm nearly to my mid-twenties, which I pray is far from the middle of my life, but lately I've been thinking a lot about dying. I know that sounds weird, and please don't think I'm depressed or anything like that, but it's just been on my mind. I haven't been thinking about how I might die as much as the fact that it's really going to happen someday. God has my life planned out, and he's already designated my last day. I kind of imagine it like a stack of sticky notes. With each day that goes by, God reaches over and peels the top note off of the stack. Sooner or later they'll all be gone.

I find myself thinking about death mostly when I am lying in bed at night. I'm thinking about my day, and I trying to determine if it really counted for anything. I think of each of those sticky notes as blank in the morning. It's my job to fill them up throughout the day. Then, at the end of the day, God files them away. Maybe on the bad days He is simply running the sticky note through the shredder.

I don't think I'm going through an early midlife crisis, but maybe I'm just starting to realize the weight of each day. With each day I am given the chance to write a page of my story. It's a struggle some days to not just sit on the couch and eat cereal in my boxers. I can't help but think that a day like that doesn't really count for anything. It's those kinds of days that get tossed in the trash.

I don't want to live a life that God looks at and wonders why He gave me so many pages. I don't want him to be disappointed due to me wasting most of them. Over the past few years and the 924 miles it took me to really start to understand life, I've actually realized I don't really understand it at all. I have, however, learned a couple of things. Though I haven't mastered this thing called life, I do know that we each have a story. I understand that God provides the blank pages that will one day sit on a shelf as our story. God lets us have the pen. He gives us the opportunity to write our stories. It's not because we can write a better story than He can, but because it's our story to write. And at the end of the day, our story will actually just be a chapter in His story. I really don't want to be the chapter in God's story that everyone skips over because it's boring or poorly written. I don't want to be the chapter that God wishes He had just cut from the book entirely.

Though I've been thinking about death and how short life is, I've realized something else. I've realized the one thing that really matters most. If we are still breathing, then God hasn't decided to end our story yet. He's still waiting for us to pick up the pen and start writing. Unless you are dead, which I imagine you aren't if you are reading this book, then you have the opportunity to begin your story today. My story started a few years ago and a half dozen states away. It took a lot of faith, courage, and a bit of chance to end up where I am today. There weren't a lot of easy decisions to make, nor did they always work out. I've never watched a movie or read a book where everything went perfectly and every gamble paid off. That wouldn't be a good movie. It wouldn't keep you on the edge of your seat.

My advice is that you pick up the pen and start writing. You don't have to know what direction to head, and you don't have to know how to write. If you are living a good story, then you will be able to write a good story. If you aren't living a good story, then you need to start. Don't be the chapter in God's story that could have been cut out without affecting the way the story ends.

Acknowledgements

This book took a lot of effort from a lot of people. I'd like to thank my wife and children for supporting me throughout writing this book and for allowing me the countless hours spent writing. I'd like to thank my parents who have taught me the meaning of giving my all, and who encouraged me to tell my story.

I'd like to thank Westbow Press for coaching me through the writing process and helping me make this book a success. I'd like to thank J.J. Murray for coaching me and helping me with some of the critical decision making for the book. I'd like to thank the people around me who are the said "village" that it takes to make this thing called life happen more smoothly. I'd like to thank everyone who stood beside me when I decided to start this book and kept me from throwing in the towel. It's people like Adam, and others who taught me that it's not just important to have a good story, but you find purpose in telling it. There are countless other people who don't even know that they influenced this book, but without them I might not have had the words to write it.

I also owe Bill Coleman for helping me in getting this book ready for press. While on a trip to Vietnam, he took the time to proofread and edit the manuscript all free of charge. For that, I am thankful.

I'd like to thank Daniel Ryan Day for his help, influence, and friendship, along with his guidance along the way. You can pick up a copy of his book, *10 Days Without,* in book stores everywhere.

I'd like to thank Patrick Childers, whose photographs that were taken while in Peru, influenced an entire chapter of this book and I'd like to thank him for letting me use his photograph of a street dog in my story. I'd also like to thank Jonathan Neeley, owner of Neeley Photography, for providing my photo shoot for the book. You can find his work on social media at his webpage, www.facebook.com/neeleyphoto.

Thank you to all of you who picked this book among millions of other possible good reads and helped me make this dream come true. Until next time, go and live a story worth telling.

Street Dogs.
Photo by Patrick Childers. Taken in Peru.

Bonus Chapter

A Pocket Full of Quarters

From: *Unscripted: Living a Good Story without Putting on a Show. (To be released)*

Sometimes we make things into something they're not. We spend so much time building a stage, making sure the lighting is right, and practicing our lines, that we forget to experience things. We forget to just be who we are.

As a writer, I get to sit in front of a screen and express myself. If I don't like the way something comes out, I just hit delete or change up the wording. Writers often are seen as introverts who write because they have trouble communicating with people. For me, that isn't it at all. I love talking to people and making new friends. I'm not good at public speaking, but if you put me in a small group setting, I can entertain the room. I think this is because I can just be myself in those settings. If you tell me that I've got to give a speech and you give me a month to prepare, then I'll most likely screw something up.

The same goes with writing. I can try and force a topic onto the page, or outline a book. Sometimes I try to force a successful writing session. When I do this, I normally end the day without any real progress. Instead, I sit at the computer and try to remember stories that are worth telling. I try to recall human experiences that will speak to other people. It took me a while to learn this principle. It took even longer to learn that knowing what your gift is doesn't mean you know how to apply it to life.

I've mentioned before that I used to plan community outreaches at a church. One of the outreaches that I planned involved going to a laundromat and paying for people to wash their clothes. We took bottled water to hand out, and we took quarters. I remember trying to plan the outreach perfectly. It was for our student ministry, so I spent a lot of time trying to find scripture that the students could share with the people at the laundromat. I tried to think of ways to teach the students to spark conversations with people.

Before we went inside to start paying for people's laundry, I remember giving a speech to the students. I explained how we could slip scripture into the conversations and how to share Christ with the people. I even told them to make sure that they explained that we were from the church down the road. Everything was planned out perfectly. That was the first problem we ran into. We were trying to force the situation to turn out a certain way.

We stayed at the laundromat for most of the day. We helped people fold their clothes, we fed the hungry machines pockets full of quarters, and we got to meet a lot of really awesome people. I don't recall telling anyone the name of our church or playing the Jesus card. I had planned to do just that, but thank God, He had a better plan. We talked about life. We talked about the things that mattered to these people. We talked about cars that weren't running well and bills that weren't getting paid on time. We talked about family and friends. We talked about life in general. I remember one lady very well. She was ninety-one years old. I sat and listened to her tell stories for over an hour. She taught me more about life than I taught her. I listened with the kind of excitement a kid has while waiting to rip into a present on Christmas morning.

We prayed with people, not because we had played the church card, but because these people had really opened up to us. They could tell we were genuine. We cried, we laughed, and we made memories that would reach further than that afternoon. At the end of the day, we had done so much more than put on a community outreach. We had made friends. We had really connected on a deeper level. We had loved them and they had loved us back. We had become a part of these people's lives in a way that was so uncommon that it seemed surreal. We hadn't been the *Jesus Promoters* that we thought we had to be in order to change people's lives. We simply became Jesus to people we met that day, and in a way they had been Jesus to us. They had demonstrated a love and acceptance that I imagine Christ would have had for everyone he met. We were on their turf, inserting ourselves into their day, and they didn't want us to leave when it was over. I had intended to teach the students how to reach out and love people. Instead, the people we met taught them more than I had ever taught them in my time at the church. It was amazing.

It was after that outreach that I realized that we didn't need a game plan in order to love people. We don't have to have a pocket full of Christian literature. We don't have to come up with some pitch in order to start a conversation. All we have to do is share in the human experience with other people.

For me, that means just writing what I feel. It means sharing stories that changed my life in hopes that it changes someone else's life too. Depending on what your gift is, it could be just as simple. My point is that we don't have to do so much planning. I don't have to outline my book before I can write it. I just have to start writing. I have to get rid of the stereotypes and the expectations that other people have set for me. I just have to be honest with people. Sometimes it just takes a story, and sometimes it doesn't require any words at all. Other times it just takes a pocket full of quarters.